The Home Adventure Library

3

People and Places

BY DAVID JOHNSTONE AND GORDON G. DUPEE

Illustrated by Seymour Fleishman

America's Story

BY PAUL NEIMARK

Illustrated by Dick Fickle

The Southwestern Company

Nashville, Tennessee

Copyright © 1984, 1982, 1979, 1973, 1968 by
The Southwestern Company
Printed in the United States of America
R.R.D.

CONTENTS

People and Places

3

America's Story

America's Story *continued*

People
and Places

The Wonderful World of Today

RAYMOND HAND, JR.

THE WORLD OF TODAY is full of wonderful things to do, interesting places to visit, and many different kinds of people to meet and to get to know.

America is a big place, with many fascinating things to see. You might travel by car to see them, or perhaps by train or bus. You could even fly in a jet airplane that would carry you along very fast, way up in the sky where the clouds are.

There are other places you could visit too, far-away lands where the people speak other languages and have different ways of living. Wouldn't it be fun to travel

5

around the world to all of those distant countries and see their interesting buildings, mighty rivers, and towering mountains?

Why don't you take a wonderful trip right now? All you need is your imagination.

Ready?

First stop: New York City, one of the great cities of the world. New York is known especially for its many tall buildings. They are called skyscrapers because they appear to touch the sky. One of the best known is the Empire State Building. It has 102 stories and is 1,250 feet tall.

Elevators whisk you up to the top in no time at all. There, you can look out at the bustling city and see the great ships coming and going in New York Harbor.

While you're in New York, why not visit the United Nations, where you can find people from nearly every country of the world. Their job is to discuss ways to solve problems and settle disagreements in a peaceful way.

Next stop: Washington, D.C., our nation's capital. Here you will surely want to visit the White House, where the President and his family live, and the Capitol Building, where Congress meets to make our laws. Your next visit will be to the Washington Monument, a tower so tall that it looks like a giant stone needle. This monument was built to honor George Washington, the first President of the United States. Another stop in your trip is the Lincoln Memorial, which has a large statue of Abraham Lincoln, the President who guided our country through the terrible years of the Civil War. The statue shows Lincoln seated in a large chair. As you look at his face, its strong, sad expression will remind you of how hard it is to be President of a great country.

Next stop: Disneyworld. This amusement park, which is in Orlando, Florida, is full of interesting and entertaining things for you to see and do. While in Orlando, you will also want to visit EPCOT Center, a sort of experimental community that will show you how people may live in the future.

From Florida you will go to New Orleans, Louisiana. If you are there in late winter, you may want to join in the Mardi Gras celebration. During Mardi Gras, people dress up in colorful and sometimes strange costumes. They dance and sing in the houses and streets. It's just like a big costume party—and all of us are invited.

New Orleans is located at the mouth of the Mississippi River, so while you are there, why not take a ride up the river on a paddle wheel steamboat. Years ago many of these wooden steamboats traveled up and down the great river, blowing their steam whistles and stopping at cities and towns along the way to pick up or drop off passengers and cargo. Now most of the wooden steamboats are gone, replaced by big steel ships. But what a joy it is for you to ride on the old paddle wheel and see the sunlight shimmering on the water and hear the swish of the wheel in the river.

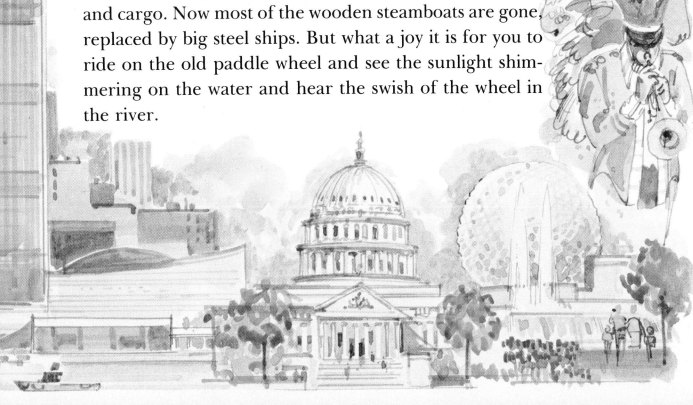

Next stop: Grand Canyon, in Arizona, truly one of the marvels of nature. The Grand Canyon was cut into the earth by the Colorado River and is a mile deep and very large. As you stand above it, on either side below you, you see steep walls of rock, whose many layers have different colors and make the canyon walls look like earth rainbows. The Colorado River is so far beneath you that it looks like a tiny stream.

Another wonder of nature is the redwood forest in California, so it's your next stop. Here you see giant redwood trees. Some of them are thought to be 2,000 years old or more, and are so big that tunnels can be cut through their mighty trunks to make way for roads. Yet the trees themselves continue to grow a little bit each year.

Next stop: Mexico, the first foreign country on your world tour. Here you may visit the ruins of Chichén Itzá. This ancient city was built by the Mayans long before Columbus discovered America.

Next you visit Machu Pichu, in the mountains of Peru in South America. This ancient, abandoned city was built long ago by a people known as the Inca, but it was not rediscovered until 1911.

9

Now get ready for a long trip, across the Pacific Ocean to Japan. This nation, which is made up of several islands, has many mountains. You will surely want to see the largest and most beautiful, Fujiyama. Mount Fuji, as it is sometimes called, is a sacred place to the Japanese, and its beauty has inspired many generations of Japanese poets and artists. Because the mountain is so tall, its top is covered with snow year round.

Next stop: China, one of the biggest countries in the world. China has more people than any other country in the world. In northern China is the Great Wall, which was built a very long time ago to keep out invading armies. As you walk along the top of the wall, remember that it is about 50 feet high, 30 feet wide, and 1,500 miles long. It would take a long time to walk the entire distance.

Ready? On to Moscow, the capital of the Soviet Union. The Soviet Union is a giant country and includes many different kinds of people, or nationalities. One of these groups is the Russians, so many people call the whole country Russia. In Moscow you can see the Kremlin, a walled group of buildings built over many years by the Russian rulers, who were known as czars. Now the Kremlin is the center of the country's government. Its many towers are crowned with round, pointed spires. These spires help give the Kremlin its special look.

On to Agra, in India, to see the Taj Mahal, one of
the world's most beautiful buildings. The Taj Mahal was
built many years ago by an Indian emperor to honor his
wife after her death. Its white marble walls have all sorts
of beautiful pictures and designs on them, made from
many small colorful stones that are set into the marble.

Next stop: Egypt, where you will visit the Pyramids. These great structures stand not far from Cairo, the capital of Egypt. The Pyramids were built a very long time ago as tombs for the Egyptian kings, who were known as Pharaohs. When they were built, the Egyptians had none of our modern machines to move the thousands of giant blocks of stone that make up the Pyramids. How the Egyptians ever built them is still one of the great wonders of all time.

Here too you see the magnificent statue of the Great Sphinx, which has the head of a person and the body of a lion.

On to Italy to visit Rome. In this old city you see the Colosseum, a giant stone stadium built by the ancient Romans. Here the gladiators—strong men—fought hand-to-hand to entertain the Romans.

Next stop: Paris, France. Paris is one of the most beautiful of Europe's great cities, as you soon find out. A good place to visit is the Louvre, one of the world's best art museums. Outside the Louvre you stand in the Tuileries, a garden with beautiful beds of flowers of every color. While in Paris, you surely want to climb the great Eiffel Tower. It stands 984 feet high and is topped by a large television antenna. The Eiffel Tower is so popular it has become a symbol for Paris itself.

Last stop on your trip: London, England. Of course, you make sure to see the changing of the guard at Buckingham Palace, the home of British kings and queens. But you also visit the building in which Parliament, the British government, meets. It is easy to recognize this building because of its big clock tower. Many times you listen to the sound of Big Ben, the giant bell in the tower, which rings out the time to all of London.

Now it is time to return home. You had fun visiting places all over the world—Disneyworld, the Grand Canyon, the Sphinx, and all the rest. But home is a special place, too, with wonders all its own.

There are supermarkets where you can buy all sorts of good things to eat, and stores where you can get clothes, books to read, toys to play with, and anything you can think of.

At home you may have all sorts of things that make our lives better—television, radio, refrigerators to keep food fresh, electric lights so we can see when it gets dark, telephones so we can talk to people any time, wherever they may be. Some people even have computers to help them in work and play.

But best of all, we have our families and good friends.

Some people here in the United States live in tall apartment buildings, where the elevators can take a person quickly from the first floor to the top floor.

Other people live in homes that have yards and trees.

There are hospitals, where sick people can get better, and there are libraries, with good books to read, records to listen to, and other things to do.

There are laboratories, where scientists study ways to make our lives better.

There are zoos full of fascinating animals, and there are museums to visit. Yes, there are lots of interesting things to see and do.

Our trip of imagination has shown us that this is a wonderful world indeed. Someday you will take a real trip and see all these places and things. You may even be one of those who will take a trip on the Space Shuttle, maybe to the Moon!

Yes, we live in a wonderful world, but life was not always exactly the way it is now. We can better understand our world of today if we look back and see how people lived long ago and how the world slowly changed and became the world we now know.

The Earliest Villages

AT FIRST, THE EARLY PEOPLE lived only in family groups—families of mothers and fathers who cared for their young. The families broke up when the children could get their own food.

Sometimes two or three families lived together or traveled together for a while. They would stop in a place where food was easy to find.

Later in man's history, many families joined together in great hunts. Once or twice a year, the people would come together from near and far. They would form a large tribe for as long as each hunt lasted. When the hunt was over, they would break up again into small families living far apart.

Many new things now happened. Wild animals, such as ponies and reindeer, were hitched to trees or kept in pens for a steady supply of meat. To feed them, grasses were planted. This was the start of herding, and the beginning of villages.

Men had learned to work together. One man could now count on the skill and strength of another. Work could be shared.

Slowly, during thousands of years, little villages of a dozen tents or huts grew on the seashores and along great rivers. Some of these villages were hunting camps. Others were tiny towns whose people fished with hook and net.

Sometimes these villagers hunted bear, and sometimes they hunted men. Each little camp or village was a whole world in itself, and any stranger was dangerous.

The herding of animals, the start of farming, the first year-round camps and villages made great changes in how people lived.

It became the duty of men and women to stay close to crops and flocks, rather than to roam out alone for food. This was a safer life, with less danger from wild animals or accidents. The change in the way of living brought people closer together, and they could learn from one another.

First Cities

THE IDEA OF CITY living is a very old one. When people settled in one place and started farming, food supplies increased tremendously. With more food, the number of people also grew quickly. Small villages soon became large towns.

Cities were built first in the warm belt of the northern hemisphere. There grain could be harvested two and three times a year, instead of only once. Great rivers supplied the water for growing crops.

Religion was very important in the lives of the people of these ancient cities. All parts of life were

thought to be directed by higher powers or *gods*. The cities were just as much centers of worship as they were markets for trade and places to live.

Because the sun was so important to farming, the sun often became the chief god of an early city. Whether the city was located in Egypt, Babylonia, China or Peru, the king was considered either the child of the sun or the sun itself. As king and chief priest, he had his people build great temples to honor the gods.

The temples of these cities were often large "sun-dials," made to show positions of the sun. The sun, as seen from the temple on a certain day of the year, would tell the city that it was time for the river's flood or time to start planting or harvesting the crops.

The king and his priests spent their lives in ruling others and worshipping the gods. As part of their worship, the priests watched natural happenings and developed such sciences as counting, arithmetic, and astronomy, the study of the stars.

Some of the earliest cities were built from 5,000 to 6,000 years ago along the Nile River in Egypt, between the Tigris and the Euphrates Rivers in Iraq, and along

21

the Ganges River in India. A little later, cities were built near the rivers of China. In the Americas, cities first appeared 1,000 to 4,000 years ago—long before Columbus. These great cities were mostly in Mexico and South America.

Strangely enough, cities were latecomers to the rice-rich lands of southeast Asia like Vietnam, Cambodia, and Laos. There they were built by the "brown" people of Cambodia about 1,000 years ago.

Some of the ancient cities were fairly large, many with populations of 40,000 to 60,000.

In addition to the king and his priests who were the rulers, there were many other kinds of people in the city. There were merchants who sold or traded foods, skins, and animals. Often these merchants organized journeys by land and sea to other cities to barter their goods. Soldiers lived in the city to protect it from attacks by outsiders. Engineers guided the flow of river waters to the farmlands. Writers or scribes recorded business deals. Artists and craftsmen made decorations and furniture for temples and homes. Slaves and servants did household work.

The ancient city in its time was as busy a place as the modern city of today.

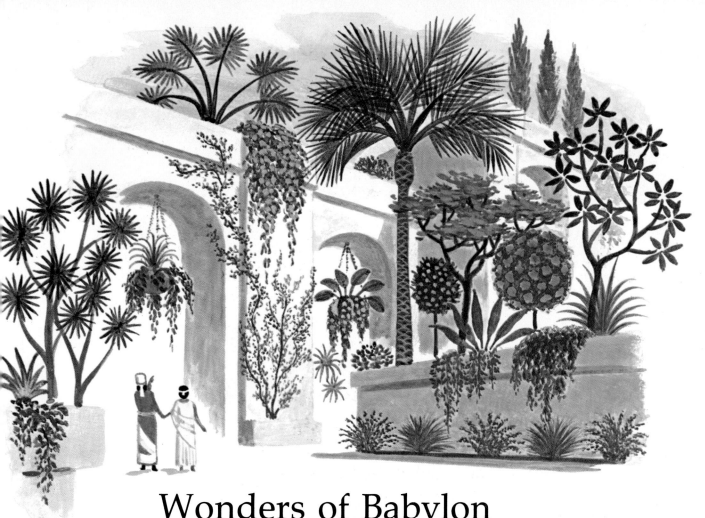

Wonders of Babylon

IT IS A GOOD THING that nobody told the makers of Babylon not to play in the mud—otherwise the city would never have been built.

In the land between the Tigris and Euphrates Rivers in the Near East, there are no trees. Babylon could not be made of wood. There are no cliffs of granite or sandstone. Babylon could not be made of rock. But there is mud. The two rivers carry tons of it into the Persian Gulf each year.

The mud of Babylon is a very special kind of clay. When it dries in the sun, it turns into hard tile.

This glorious ancient city, placed on a wide river between flat land and mountain, desert and farm, started life as a trading post. For 1,000 years, buying and selling were important parts of Babylon's life.

From the farms around Babylon came barley and wheat. Wheat was cut with a clay sickle, then ground and baked into bread. Besides planting wheat and barley, the farmers tended cows, donkeys, sheep and goats. These they brought into the town to sell to the hungry city-dwellers for silver. The farmers in turn used silver to buy cloth and pottery.

City merchants of Babylon sent the farm products by caravan across the plain and into the mountains to other lands where food was needed. The caravans also carried the work of the city's craftsmen: carved gems,

an art which the Babylonians mastered early; cloth of wool; and copper utensils. Trading boats traveled down the rivers carrying still more goods.

Into Babylon came building stones from the mountains of Lebanon, smelted copper from northern Arabia, timber from the Persian Gulf, gold and uncut jewels from the Negev desert in the south of Palestine.

To keep records of their business, the merchants of Babylon invented writing—a peculiar form of writing done by pressing the tip of a reed into wet clay. They also invented arithmetic.

The Babylonians were famous for their laws. At first laws were set up to make sure each farmer got a fair share of water. Later, laws were established to settle differences between tradesmen.

A famous king of Babylon, Hammurabi, started life as a soldier. After 30 years as a desert warrior, Hammurabi conquered Babylon and became its king. He then made laws which helped people live together happily. The laws of Hammurabi eased punishment for many crimes and gave protection to those owing money.

Because the city was a wealthy trading center, it was necessary to build defenses against invaders.

One of the chief wonders of ancient Babylon was its great walls, all made of clay brick. The outer wall of the city was between 42 and 56 miles long, 85 feet thick, and as high as a four-story building. There were one hundred bronze gates. In front of the wall was a deep moat, or water-filled ditch.

One of the kings of Babylon married a princess from the mountain country. To ease her longing for home, he built the Hanging Gardens of Babylon. The gardens were built on top of arches 75 feet tall, with plants from all over the known world. Among the plants brought in for the gardens, it is said, was a cotton "tree." Soon cotton became an important crop in the Near East and Egypt.

The Babylonians were very religious and built great brick towers as temples for their gods. Often these towers faced east—toward the exact point where the sun rose on the day of the river's flood. The farmers then knew that more water was coming and could guide it through their fields to water the crops.

The Babylonians invented the sundial, which told the hour of the day from the shadow cast by the sun. They used lenses of crystal to study the stars.

Ancient Egypt

BECAUSE THE EGYPTIANS took special care of their dead, we know more about them than about any other ancient people. The hot, dry winds from the deserts on each side of the Nile River valley have been of great help, too. They have preserved many colorful paintings of ancient Egyptian life.

Egypt, like Babylonia, combined bright, active living under a hot sun with a rather gloomy religion. The many Egyptian gods were often shown as animals. The "heaven" of the Egyptians was a number of bad places full of monster snakes and crocodiles.

The story of Egypt is the story of its river. The flooding of the Nile made farming—and living—possible. Every year, the Nile flooded and covered the land with deep, rich soil brought from inner Africa.

As the early Egyptian cities grew, the priests who were in charge of giving water to the farms became more and more powerful. Soon the entire country was under control of one person, called the Pharaoh. Originally a priest, the Pharaoh came to be worshipped as a god.

When most people think of the Pharaohs of Egypt, they think of the pyramids. There are three pyramids, which are great piles of stone built to protect a dead Pharaoh and the treasures buried with the Pharaoh.

Because the ancient Egyptians believed that the bodies of the dead went to heaven, they did all they could to preserve them. With the dead, they buried honey and grain for the soul to use as food.

The largest pyramid was built by the Pharaoh Cheops (or Khufu) in 3,733 B.C. It was 450 feet tall. In all, this great pyramid is said to weigh almost five million tons. To build it, more than 100,000 people worked for many years.

The large sandstone blocks used to build the pyramids were found in Upper Egypt. They were dragged on huge rollers to the river. There they were placed on barges and pulled upstream.

Nobody knows how the large blocks were placed in position. It is thought that large earth ramps were built, and the blocks pulled up on rollers.

The great pyramid of Cheops contains burial rooms at its center. Beautiful paintings, jewelry, and vases have been found. Today scientists are studying the great pyramid to see if more chambers are inside it.

Many of the great temples and statues of Egypt are now disappearing under water. The government of Egypt has built a high dam at Aswan so that the Egyptian farmers may have water the year around. The building of the dam has flooded the land behind it, drowning many treasures of the past. Some have been saved by being moved to higher ground.

The Persian Conqueror

FROM TIME TO TIME in history, there have been leaders who could bring together many people in a single cause.

Such a man was Cyrus, leader of the Persians.

The Persians were farmers and shepherds living in mountain valleys north of the Persian Gulf. They had no wealth, no writing, no art. They were ruled by people called the Medes, who lived to the north.

The Persians tended their small farms, cared for their sheep, and dreamed of the past glories of the old Persian empire. They also improved their skill with the

30

bow and arrow. One of these mountain valley tribes finally formed a small kingdom called Anshan.

The man called Cyrus became king of Anshan. Very little is known of his early life, but he must have come from among those tribes who were skilled with the bow and arrow. First Cyrus united all the many Persian tribes. Within three years his new kingdom was strong enough to challenge and defeat the Medes. Soon the fame of the fast-shooting, hard-riding Persians, who triumphed under clouds of arrows, spread throughout the countries in the Near East.

Having defeated the Medes, the Persians were ready to conquer other lands. As rough tribes always do, they dreamed of winning the wealth of great cities.

The richest nation known to the Persians was a country on their western border called Lydia. According to legend, Croesus, the king of Lydia, was the wealthiest man in the world. He was said to have started the coining of money. Dressed in his rough leather pants, Cyrus assembled his armies of tribesmen and crossed the border to invade Lydia.

The strongest part of the Lydian army was the horse troops. Knowing that horses hate and fear the smell of camels, Cyrus brought up camels from the rear and placed them in the front of his attacking army. The Lydian horses, smelling the camels, broke and ran. Cyrus won the battle.

Cyrus next turned to the great city of Babylon. After defeating troops of the Babylonian king, Belshazzar, he entered the city without resistance.

Three years after Cyrus was killed in battle, his son Cambyses conquered Egypt. Now the Persian empire was the largest empire in the world, except for China. Its people included rich city-dwellers, mountain tribesmen, shepherds and farmers, desert warriors—people who wore turbans and people who wore lambskin hats.

The Persian empire was lucky to have still another great king, Darius. He set to work to bind together this vast empire, which stretched from the Indus River in India to the Aegean Sea. Roads were built from end to end of the great empire. Trading between all the parts of the empire grew. Royal messengers rode these highways and formed the beginnings of a mail system.

As happens with most great empires, the early great kings, such as Cyrus and Darius, were followed by others who were less daring and less skilled in ruling. After only two centuries of peace, the Persian empire crumbled and was defeated.

The Great Wall of China

WHEN THE FIRST ASTRONAUTS reached the moon, they possibly were able to see one man-made thing on Earth without a telescope . . . the Great Wall of China.

The Great Wall of China reaches 1,500 miles along the country's northern border, from the Yellow Sea's Gulf of Chihli to the western mountains. It separates China on the south from Manchuria and Mongolia on the north.

The wall is young compared with the pyramids of Egypt. It was started in 214 B.C. But it took a thousand years to finish it.

34

In its 1,500-mile length, the Great Wall rolls over the tops of hills, into deep valleys, along broad plains, and through salt marshes before reaching the coast. It is 30 feet thick and 40 to 50 feet high. Every few miles, there are towers for look-outs, and arched gates with huge doors for armies to ride through.

The purpose of the wall was to keep the northern armies of Mongols and Tartars on horseback away from the settled plains and large cities of China.

The wall was built entirely by hand. The work was hard—perhaps as hard as the building of the pyramids in Egypt. Bloodstains still show on some of the stones.

The Great Wall was built with slave labor. At first condemned criminals were used. Later, merchants and scholars who disagreed with the emperor were forced to work on the wall. Such labor also built great palaces, some with halls large enough to hold 10,000 people.

The man who started building the Great Wall of China was the Emperor Shih Huang Ti, first ruler of the Ch'in dynasty. (A *dynasty* is a family of kings.)

Although Shih was able to create one Chinese nation from many feudal states, in many ways he was a bad and cruel ruler.

When he became emperor, he announced that he had unlimited power. The scholars who ran the offices of the government protested that he was breaking the law. Shih answered them by burning all books, except those on magic, medicine, and farming. Then he put the scholars to work on the Great Wall. Many of the scholars, unused to hard physical work, died on the job.

A tomb as big as any pyramid was built for Shih in a western mountain. When it was finished, he killed all the builders, so that no one could tell the tomb's secrets or disturb his body.

An Island Kingdom

ONE OF THE FIRST Thanksgivings is pictured on a big stone jar which is 3,500 years old. The jar was not found in the land of the Pilgrims but on the sunny island of Crete. This island is halfway between Greece and Egypt in the Mediterranean Sea.

The Cretans had much to be thankful for. They could grow grain for bread without worrying about water as the Egyptians and Babylonians did. Olives grew plentifully, and the olive oil was used as butter. Grape vines, growing in the hot sun on the hillsides, became heavy with fruit. From the grapes they made wine, which was drunk as we drink coffee, tea, or milk. With plenty to eat, without a great deal of work or worry, the Cretans were a happy people. They had time to sing and dance and draw pictures.

Living in an island kingdom, the Cretans early learned to sail ships. They became great sea traders. About 2,000 years before Christ, the Cretans were trading busily with the Egyptians to the south.

In Egypt, the Cretans found the riches of civilization. They brought them home. Egyptian things were "made over" by the Cretans in their own lively style and carried northward to the rude Greek tribes.

As the rich ships of Crete sailed back and forth between Egypt and Greece, the island of Crete grew more powerful. Finally, Crete came to rule the whole

Aegean Sea, between Greece and what is now Turkey. So strong was Crete that its people thought themselves safe from attack. They built great palace-cities with only a few strong walls.

The Cretan palaces had many things which might be considered modern—great pipes of tile to carry water, furnaces for making pottery, and porcelain (or "china") wall decorations. Colorful wall paintings show that the Cretan ladies wore long, flowing skirts quite like the French fashions of Napoleon's court.

The Cretans were great sportsmen. Some of their palace cities had open-air theatres in which boxing matches were held.

But the chief sports of Crete had to do with the bull, which was a sacred animal. There were many bull

hunts. There was also a kind of bull-dance, which may be the ancestor of the Spanish and Mexican bullfights of today. Since the bull was sacred, the bull-dance was both a sport and a religious ceremony. A young boy or girl would grab the horns of a running bull and do a somersault over its back. The bull-dancers trained for years to master this sport.

This is probably the start of the legend of the Minotaur or "king-bull." The Minotaur was supposed to be a man-monster with the head of a bull. While Crete ruled the Aegean Sea, Greek cities, including Athens, were forced to send their fairest boys and girls to be fed to the Minotaur. This continued until an Athenian leader, Theseus, went to Crete and killed the monster.

The early, rough Greek tribes learned civilization from the Cretans, who carried it in their ships from Egypt to Crete to Greece. After the Greeks became civilized, they sailed to Crete and burned its palaces.

Driven from their homes by the Greeks, the Cretans moved to the coast of Asia. Some of them became the Philistines talked about in the Bible.

The Greeks
Invent Democracy

GREECE IS LIKE A HAND with many fingers, reaching down from Europe into the blue Mediterranean Sea. It is surrounded by islands, like jewels falling from the fingers of the mainland. The Mediterranean Sea seemed, to the ancient Babylonians, Persians, and Egyptians, a mighty ocean. Sailors then knew nothing of the wide Atlantic or Pacific oceans.

For centuries, rough tribes came down from the north, like waves washing over the land of Greece. Greece was a land of many mountains with wide, fertile plains between them. There the invading tribesmen

found grapes and olives growing under sunny skies. These wandering tribes stopped, tilled the land, put sheep to graze, and grew more grape vines and olive trees, along with wheat on the grassy plains.

As tribes settled in the many plains between the many mountain ranges, they built cities. They also made laws to rule those who lived in and around the cities. Each city had its own laws. These cities were called *city-states*. Two of the largest and most powerful of the city-states were Athens and Sparta.

While Cyrus and Darius were building the Persian empire, the people of Athens, the Athenians, were building great outdoor theaters, writing plays and poetry, composing music, and building temples to their gods. Many of these great marble temples still stand today, after more than 2,000 years. And many of the plays are still performed, in theaters everywhere.

The Greeks believed their gods lived on top of a high, snow-capped mountain, far to the north. It was called Mount Olympus.

Today, many a boy and girl dreams of becoming an athlete and competing in the Olympic Games. So did the children of Athens. The first Olympic Games were held in Athens more than 2,000 years ago. To start those first games, swift runners carried a fiery torch from Mount Olympus to Athens. The flame was kept burning until the games ended.

Even today the Olympic Games are started with runners bringing a lighted torch all the way from Greece. Sometimes that flame is brought more than halfway around the world — to Berlin, Tokyo, Rome, Mexico City — wherever the games are now held.

The Greeks left us not only the Olympic Games but an idea very important to our modern world —

democracy. *Democracy* is a Greek word. It means "rule by the people." In Athens this did not mean rule by all the people. Women and slaves could not vote.

Even so, the idea that many people should rule began in Athens. This was quite different from the rule of the Egyptian kings or Cyrus of Persia, or from the one-man rule in Babylon and China.

To the Athenians, democracy was more than a way of ruling. It was a way of living. Unlike their Persian neighbors, who were still dressed in leather pants and lambskin caps, the people of Athens loved beauty, games, and their freedom.

The Athenians became fine metal workers, potters, and weavers. They also had oil from olives and wine from grapes. All these things were traded in the open, sunny market squares of Athens and other city-states. Fleets of ships carried these things to the coasts of Italy, southern Europe, and the eastern shores of the Mediterranean.

As Athens grew rich, its free people had time to think. Some of the greatest thinkers of ancient times were Athenians. Such men as Socrates, Plato, and Aristotle, who are called *philosophers*, were Athenian teachers. They held classes under trees, on street corners, or in the market squares. Their students were young men of Athens and men from far distant cities. The king of Macedon sent his son, Alexander, to Athens to study with Aristotle.

The fall of Greece began when the two largest city-states began to war against each other. Athens and Sparta were natural enemies.

While the Athenians lived a life of freedom, wealth, and art, the Spartans lived a life of hardship. They honored the brave and the strong and the silent. They had no time for architects, sculptors, musicians, thinkers, or writers of plays. One of their heroes was a boy who stole and hid a little fox under his coat. Rather than tell what he had done, he let the fox eat his stomach!

Sparta finally defeated Athens. But to the north a new people, the Macedonians, became the enemy of all the cities of Greece.

Their leader and ruler was Alexander, who had been a student of Aristotle of Athens! He and his armies not only conquered all of Greece but also defeated the Persian Empire. Soon Alexander's kingdom stretched from India in the east, through Greece, and across the Mediterranean to Egypt.

Many great empires have risen and fallen in the long history of man. Athens, however, even though defeated by others, left for us writings, buildings, laws, and ways of governing. The Greeks made a mark in history that few people have ever equaled.

The Romans
Build Roads and Bridges

LONG AGO, EUROPE was a place of wandering tribes who lived in forests, on river banks, or by the seashore. The real growth of modern Europe was started by the Romans.

Rome began as a small trading town in Italy. On either side were tribes of Latins and tribes of Etruscans. Rome was a cluster of small huts on the edge of a swamp. Its people were outcasts from other tribes. They lived as farmers, shepherds, and traders.

The Romans always had a great love of their city. Those who first founded Rome were later worshipped

as gods. They were supposed to have been two babies left in the woods to die, who were found and raised by a wolf. These brothers, Romulus and Remus, gave Rome its name.

The very early Rome—a town between tribes usually at war with one another—soon learned to fight well, too. In time the Romans absorbed the Latins and Etruscans, their warring neighbors. From the Latins they got the name of their language, Latin.

Much later, Latin grew into French, Italian, Spanish, and many other languages. Still other languages "borrowed" Latin words. As you grow older, you will be surprised to find how many English words you use began with those Romans!

As Rome expanded through its wars, the city changed. Soldiers became more and more important. Rome was no longer a group of huts on the edge of a marsh. Rome was now a great city. The rich people grew richer, and the poor lost their old protections. Battles between the rich and the poor began. The rich were usually the descendants of the early settlers. The poor were the new arrivals. Out of these conflicts Rome changed from a republic to a city ruled by one strong man.

The Roman leader that we perhaps know most about was Julius Caesar, one of the world's greatest generals. Caesar was a noble who took the side of the poor. He was chosen to lead the Roman armies on an invasion into Gaul (the land that is modern France). He conquered Gaul and even invaded England. Then he returned to Rome.

Back in Rome with his triumphant armies, Julius Caesar took the office of *tribune*. The tribune's job was to protect the poor from the rich. The tribune was free from arrest. He could himself free any person imprisoned. He was above the law in many ways.

Later, Caesar had himself made "dictator"—at first for ten years, later for life. The Roman Senate watched as he took over more of their powers.

Some of the nobles feared that freedom in Rome was dying. They murdered Caesar on the steps of the Senate building. One of the assassins was a close friend, Brutus. Brutus thought more deeply of his country than he did of friendship.

The murder did not solve anything for long. Caesar's nephew, Augustus, took over the armies and had himself named emperor.

Under the emperors, Rome rose to its greatest glory. It soon became master of all the great cities of Europe, North Africa, and the Near East.

As the Romans conquered, they left behind roads upon which the armies had moved. They left bridges used by the armies to cross rivers and conquer more land. High stone water troughs for irrigation, called aqueducts, are still standing. Temples and theaters mark where the Romans marched and conquered.

Perhaps even more lasting were the laws the Romans made, first for themselves, then for others. These laws brought order to the rough tribes of early Europe.

Rome grew to be one of the most beautiful cities of the world. But it was also a city of great contrasts. While the poor could not get enough grain for bread, the rich ate peacocks and even ice cream, which was snow brought from the mountain-tops and sweetened.

The Roman emperors constantly tried to please the people to keep them happy. Spectacular circuses were held in a great arena. There were chariot races, and fights to the death between men and between men and wild animals.

As the empire grew larger, it became more difficult to rule. Finally, it broke into two parts. The western half had Rome as its capital. Constantinople was the eastern capital, and another emperor ruled there.

The emperors could no longer depend on the Romans to be soldiers. They had to rely on tribesmen around the empire's borders. These lean, hard peoples learned of the wealth of Rome and planned to take it for themselves.

In 476 A.D., the western empire, in Rome, fell to the Huns and Germans who invaded from the north. The Dark Ages of Europe began. The eastern empire lasted a thousand years more before falling to the Arabs and Turks.

The Huns, the Goths
and Darkness

MORE THAN 2,100 YEARS AGO, the Chinese began building a great wall to keep invaders out. But this wall did not keep the Chinese in. As they grew in numbers, the Chinese pushed westward beyond their Great Wall. There, on the wide, grassy plains of Russia in middle Asia, they met the Mongols and the Huns.

The Mongols and Huns were fierce, hard-riding tribes of horsemen. Most of the Mongols joined the Chinese. There was not enough room for all three tribes. And so most of the Huns were pushed westward into Europe. They finally reached what we now call Germany.

The fierce invasion of the Huns now forced the Germans
—or Goths—to move away and seek new lands. The
German tribes turned south.

Led by Alaric, a soldier who had been trained
by the Romans, the Goths invaded Italy. The Roman
Empire was weak now. The bearded Goths—called
"barbarians" by the clean-shaven Romans—won easily.
They burned part of Rome in 410 A.D. Then they
moved on.

The Goths had always led a simple, rustic life. Their palaces were timber houses, enclosed by stockades. They ate meat from animals they had hunted in the cold, dark, northern forest. Their plates were made of wood. In Rome they saw marble palaces and paved streets. Roman nobles were served by slaves, and ate from plates of gold and silver.

Later, under Attila the Hun, a second wave of Goths invaded Italy, conquered the Gauls in France, and invaded Spain.

What was the result of this invasion by the barbarians? People who study history call it the "Dark Ages." One historian tells us that very few people in all Europe could read or write. Until about the year 1100, ignorance was king, and darkness ruled. The great centers of learning—Carthage, Rome, Alexandria, Milan—all had been destroyed by the roving barbarians.

In the Dark Ages trade came almost to a standstill. There was little money. There were few things to sell. The only ships afloat were those of pirates, who raided villages on the coast. Roman law and Roman government were gone. A man might be killed in trying to walk to the next town.

What was left?

A way of life called *feudalism*. Almost every man and his family were tied to the land and to the land's master. The master was usually a soldier. The master-soldier told the people, "Pay me with most of your produce, and I will guard you from enemies. If you don't pay me, I will beat you and kill you." He sold protection. In this way he grew rich and strong, and the

people on the land grew weak and poor. Soon the master-soldier became a noble, then a prince, then a king, ruling the land around his castle. The people on the land stayed poor.

In the Dark Ages, lands and people that had been ruled by Roman law were plunged into chaos. Courts of law, as we know them today, and as the Romans had known them, were gone.

In place of law, men had strange ways to settle their differences. One way was for a man to swear he was telling the truth, and to get as many friends as he could to do the same. It was thought that if people did not swear truly, divine forces would punish them. Therefore, the man who could get the most people to swear he was telling the truth was right!

In the Dark Ages, children did not go to school. In fact, there were no schools. From their earliest years, children worked just as their mothers and fathers did.

These centuries after the fall of Rome were dark in many other ways. Without learning, more and more people came to believe in silly things. They believed in ghosts and witches. They believed that some people turned into wolves and other wild animals. Today we call such beliefs "superstitions."

When one looks back upon the Great Pyramids of Egypt, the Hanging Gardens of Babylon, the freedom of Athens, and the laws and roads and bridges that spread from Rome, it is easy to see why the centuries after the fall of Rome seemed to be such Dark Ages.

The Desert People

IN THE DESERT LANDS of Arabia there lived two kinds of people. One kind lived in cities or in towns where trading caravans passed. The other kind of Arab was the desert shepherd.

Arabia is a vast stretch of land between the Red Sea and the Persian Gulf, with the Indian Ocean on the south. There are no rivers in Arabia. City dwellers lived near the oceans. The shepherds wandered in the interior desert.

The desert shepherd, called the Bedouin, had a large family and often raided other families. The

attacks were more like football games than anything else. The prize to the winner was usually livestock! Today, most Bedouins live in Saudi Arabia.

In the beginning of the Arabian nation, there were often bad feelings between the city-dwellers and those who roamed the sandy desert hills. Even today, many parts of the Arab world have a hard time getting along with each other.

Though the first Arabs fought among themselves, as they still do, they were united in one religion. Their prophet was named Mohammed. His followers were called Mohammedans or *Moslems*. Mohammed was both prophet and king, ruler and religious leader.

Within one hundred years after his death, the united, religious armies of the Arabs had swept Syria, Persia, Armenia, Iraq, Egypt, and the whole of North Africa. All was conquered in the name of Allah, the Moslem God. The empire of *Islam*, another name for the religion of Mohammed, spread east to the edge of India.

In 792, a century after Mohammed's death, Baghdad became the capital of the Moslem empire.

58

Baghdad was near where ancient Babylon had stood, on the Tigris River. It is said that at its greatest, Baghdad was five miles wide and had more than two million people living within its walls.

Out of this wealthy city came such famous tales as "Aladdin and the Magic Lamp," "Sinbad the Sailor," and "Ali Baba and the Forty Thieves."

When the Arabs conquered North Africa they found another desert, with more desert people. These desert people, the Berbers, accepted the Islamic faith. In time, the empire was extended across the Straits of Gibraltar. The faith of Mohammed reached deep into Spain.

When Europe was in the Dark Ages, the Arab civilization reached its highest in Spain. The Arab, or Moorish, center of Spain was Cordova. This was soon a city of half a million people. It had grand palaces and 300 public baths. In Cordova alone, there were 3,000 *mosques*, the name for a Moslem place of worship. When only a handful of churchmen in all Europe could read and write, the University of Cordova had thousands of students. At that time in history, the tenth century, Cordova was a city of wealth and learning unequaled in the whole world.

Europe owes a debt to the Arabs, or Moors. It was they who brought to Spain, and kept alive, much of Greek and Hebrew learning. When Europe reawakened from the Dark Ages, it found treasures of the past in the Moorish cities of Spain.

Men of the Bays

MEN HAVE WANDERED all over the world for many reasons. They wandered in search of food. They wandered out of curiosity—they wanted to know what lay beyond the hills. When they reached the water's edge, again they grew curious about what lay over the water. They set sail to find new lands.

People from Denmark and islands in the North Sea moved in boats to southern England. They must have found some of the roads and buildings left by the Romans. These Danes and others were followed by the Vikings or "men of the bays."

The Vikings came from Denmark, Sweden, and the mountain bays of Norway. The ones who invaded England were mostly younger men who had no land to cultivate at home. They had to venture upon the sea. In their homeland, they often had to travel by boat from one farm to another. They had become fine seamen and good fighters.

Vikings conquered the eastern half of England, won Normandy in France, and settled Iceland. At the same time, other Norsemen traveled into Russia. There they became the fathers of the Russian czars.

The Viking longboat, driven by oars and carrying sails, left home in the summer. The longboats rode the waves like sea gulls.

Longboats carried Vikings to Iceland late in the ninth century. The Vikings mixed there with the Irish. They, too, were great sailors, who had discovered the island earlier.

A Viking from Iceland, Erik the Red, discovered Greenland a century later. It is said that Erik went to sea to avoid punishment for the death of a man. About fifteen years later, Eric's son, Leif the Lucky, was blown off course while heading for Greenland. He landed somewhere in America. The land he found was rich with "grapes and self-grown wheat." Leif named it Vinland, for the many vines.

Some say Leif's "Vinland" was Nova Scotia in Canada. Others believe it was what we now call Rhode Island. Still others think it may have been Cape Cod, Massachusetts.

The stories of these early voyages to America are told in the Icelandic *sagas* or poems. These poems tell of brawling companies of sailors traveling great distances in their small boats.

On arriving at Vinland, the Vikings fought with the Indians (or Eskimos, who may have lived farther south in those days). The Vikings called these people "shrillers," because they couldn't understand their fast, shrill speech.

In Vinland, the Vikings built a camp of log huts. Some of the huts were used to store their boats, which were pulled up on land for the winter. During the winter they hunted, and in the spring they set forth again for home, carrying a load of logs.

Neither Greenland nor Iceland had many trees, but when the ship-building Vikings discovered America, they found all the forests they could use.

Some believe the Vikings sent expeditions out of Vinland up the Hudson River in New York and down the St. Lawrence River to the Great Lakes and Minnesota. But there is no proof of this. Except for a few loads of wood, the Vikings got little from America.

The Incas

HIGH IN THE MOUNTAINS of Peru and Bolivia, in South America, an ancient people called the Incas built a great empire. They built it long before Columbus set sail from Spain in search of an ocean passage to the riches of India and the East.

The Incas did not have much farm land, except in a few valleys between high mountains. Those who lived in the mountains built *terraces*, or "shelves" of land, on the mountain sides. There they grew crops. These terraces on the mountain sides were so important that it was the Inca rulers' duty to help build them.

In the land of the Incas, the common man could not be made a slave. He and his family were treated very well by the rulers. Work depended on age. Children played freely until they were 5 years old. Boys and girls from 5 to 9 did housework. Youngsters of 9 to 16 served as shepherds for the flocks of llamas that grazed in the mountains. The hard work of farming was done by men and women. Old people were given light work to keep them busy and useful. In all Peru, there were no beggars.

While the Incas cared very well for their own people, they were organized to conquer other tribes. And conquer other tribes they did. The Inca empire at its greatest included the land that is now the modern

South American countries of Peru, Ecuador, Bolivia, and parts of Chile and Argentina. The empire was as large as those won by Alexander, Caesar, or Napoleon.

Like many other peoples, the Incas thought of their ruler or king as a god of the sun. They also thought that the movements of snakes and spiders could tell whether good or bad things were going to happen. In times of war, the priests would carry painted stones around a great sacred fire. These stones were painted with images of snakes and toads and jaguars.

Instead of raising sheep for wool, the Incas raised llamas, a beautiful and proud cousin of the camel. If you were to take a trip to Peru today, you would still find llamas walking in the streets and squares of

towns and cities. The wool of the llamas was very important to the Incas because the weather in the high mountains is very cold, especially at night.

The government was paid for by taxes from the people. They contributed a small portion of what they farmed or herded. Some of the men "paid" their taxes in work—building the terraces on the mountain sides, building roads, or making rope bridges across the mountain canyons.

Runners were hired by the government to carry the "mail"—messages made by knotting strings. The place of the knots on the string gave the meaning. So swift were these runners that they could carry fresh fish from the ocean through thick jungles to the great cities in the mountains.

The Incas were great builders, as many ruins still standing today tell us. They learned to bind together the stones of their great buildings and temples with copper clamps. Peru is still rich in copper and gold.

In medicine, the Incas developed a way of cutting through the living human skull. They probably did this operation to let out evil spirits from the heads of the sick.

When the Spaniards came to the New World, after the voyages of Columbus, the Inca empire was plundered and destroyed. Its gold was taken to Spain. Only a few ruins remain today to tell us how great the Inca empire was.

Europe Reawakens

IN AN ODD WAY, much of our modern world has come from a rat. Let's look at this idea for a moment.

The rat lived somewhere in central Asia. He climbed aboard a visiting ship that was carrying cargo to Italy. He got off the ship at the Italian city of Genoa in 1347.

On the back of this rat was a flea. The flea carried the germs of the "Black Death," a plague. A *plague* is a sickness that spreads from person to person, from place to place. The Black Death was one of the worst things ever to happen to man. It killed about one-third of all the people in Europe and Asia.

In China alone, 13 million died—a number equal to all the people in New York and Chicago today. Those in China who did not die were so sick they neglected to guard the river banks. Great floods poured over the rice fields. More millions drowned or starved.

In Europe, the Black Death spread from Italy to one country after another. In a little more than a year it killed 25 million people. The plague first reached England by 1348. It was worst in the large towns, where people lived closely together in poor houses with bad water and spoiled food.

With so many people dead, there were few people left to farm the lands. Landlords demanded rent that farmers could not pay. The landlords grew angry. The farmers rebelled. The rebellion started men asking questions about why all these things were happening.

Asking questions is one thing that people do and animals do not. It is one of the best things you can do. Asking questions helps people learn. Questions bring about change. In Europe, the Black Death made many, many people begin to ask many questions. These questions did away with the superstitions of the Dark

Ages. They weakened the power of the feudal lords and challenged the church.

Questioning in Europe led to the reawakening of science. Science grew and grew until man was able, not many years ago, to create a spaceship.

Of course there are many other reasons for the reawakening, or *Renaissance*, of Europe. One other reason was a very curious boy. His name was Leonardo, and he was born in Vinci, near Florence in Italy. Today we call him Leonardo da Vinci. He was one of the great painters of the world. We remember him most for his paintings called *Mona Lisa* and *The Last Supper*. Actually, Leonardo finished very few of the paintings he began. He was not lazy, just curious. He kept a notebook in which he made drawings of things that interested him.

71

He was interested in the bone structure of the human body. He was interested in plants. He was perhaps the first to describe fossils, the remains of ancient plant and animal life.

He was curious about how birds fly. He made drawings of a flying machine with great flapping wings. He designed the first war tank with guns.

The Italian city-states, like their Greek cousins centuries earlier, were bubbling with activity, trade, and ocean-going commerce. Ships carried goods and ideas to and from the Orient. Caravans carried goods and ideas north from sunny Italy to other parts of Europe and to England.

A man called Copernicus said that the earth revolved around the sun, instead of the other way around. Almost nobody believed him. But one man, Galileo, did believe him. Galileo invented the telescope, and looked at the sun and moon.

The Arabs and Moors had invaded Spain from North Africa years and years before. They brought with them the mathematics of the Near East and the learning of the Hebrews and Greeks.

The Mongols and Huns brought gunpowder from China. Gunpowder changed war, on land and sea. The Chinese had also discovered how to make paper. The printing machine was invented in Germany. Now books were being made. Books spread ideas and information.

With the printing of the Bible, people slowly began to read Christian scriptures for themselves. They were no longer completely dependent upon the church for learning about religion.

European Christians crusaded against the Moslems and Turks for control of the Holy Land. These crusades were made by thousands of people, rich and poor, who otherwise might have spent their whole lives in their own little villages. In traveling across Europe and into the Middle East, the crusaders learned and saw many things they would not have seen at home.

All these strange things—the rat, Leonardo, crusades, commerce with the far East, questioning—helped wake up Europe. Like a slumbering giant, Europe came out of darkness, perhaps never to sleep again.

The Sun Never Sets

THE LARGEST AND LAST EMPIRE in history was the only one started by a woman.

This great empire was the British Empire. It came to rule lands around the whole world. People said, "The sun never sets on the British Empire." When it was night in England, the sun was shining in Australia, one of the British colonies. When it was noon in India, a British colony, it was still night in Africa.

The British Empire got off to a good start because Queen Elizabeth the First was smart. She got the eager young men of England to do her work.

At the beginning of the sixteenth century, Spain was the great nation of the day. Spain was competing with Portugal for control of North and South America. Not a week went by but the great Spanish galleons brought gold and silver to Spain from the mines of Peru and Mexico.

Little England was unimportant, a mosquito which buzzed around the head of the Spanish king.

When Elizabeth mounted England's throne, she did not start war with Spain. Instead, she let her eager young men buy ships to attack and rob the Spanish and Portuguese merchant fleets. These English "pirate" ships sank Spanish galleons, burned Spanish towns, and won Spanish treasures. Queen Elizabeth was training a navy at no cost!

King Philip of Spain was a greedy ruler. He took the flowing wealth of the Americas for his own use. He ignored the Spanish nobles and the people in passing laws. He ruined farmers and townsmen with heavy taxes. Many wise men of learning fled from Spain and went to Holland.

On the other hand, good things were happening in little England. Ships returning from all parts of the world carried not only gold and silk and precious stones, but ideas—new ideas. An awakening in the arts and sciences was taking place.

The court of Queen Elizabeth honored the pirates who brought gold from Spanish ships. The court also honored writers like William Shakespeare. He taught the English tongue how to sing as it had never sung before.

It was a time for asking questions, a time for writing music. An apple fell from a tree, and a man began to wonder what "made" it fall. Many people were still poor, but England was growing stronger. Soon it would be much more than just a little island. From English shores ships began sailing with people who wanted to find new lands. Many came to settle in the New World, to make a New England.

At last, Philip of Spain prepared for a showdown with England. He felt he must act while he could.

In the Spanish harbors, he got ready a fleet of ships. It was called the Invincible Armada—a name that meant it could not be defeated! This fleet, which had about 150 vessels, was to carry the Spanish soldiers to invade England.

Half the Spanish ships were *galleons.* They were high, with many decks, built for running before the wind. They could not easily change direction at sea. Their guns were high above the water line for long-range firing. They were useless for close-in fighting.

The other half of the fleet was a jumble of small craft, carrying food, clothing, and other supplies.

Philip did not ask whether the captains of the fleet were good sailors. So long as they were nobles, and of the right religion, they could hold command.

The English had many advantages over the Spaniards. All the ships in the English fleet were warships. They were light and could turn quickly in any direction. They were small enough to sail under the Spanish guns without being hit. They were commanded by seasoned sailors, trained to sink galleons.

The English were not very worried. Their spies in Spain had informed them of the progress of the Armada. Watchmen posted along the British coast lit bonfires to tell the Armada's speed.

Sir Francis Drake, the English sea commander who had been a privateer, was bowling when news of the Armada came. So sure was he of English success that he finished his game before putting to sea!

The Spanish Armada sailed up the English Channel in a great half-moon, seven miles from tip to tip.

The Channel between France and Britain is narrow, shallow and treacherous. Drake allowed the Armada to proceed without attack. A high wind which was blowing soon turned into a full storm.

The Spanish commanders became seasick. Their ships were driven past Flanders, in Belgium. There they sought shelter in a harbor.

Then Drake attacked, sending fire-ships into the Spanish fleet, which was completely routed. The survivors of the Armada ran north around Scotland and were again caught in terrible storms in the Irish Sea. Many were shipwrecked. Only 54 ships—about a third of the Armada—reached home.

With the defeat of the Armada, Spain's command of the sea was ended. Power now passed to little England. It was the real beginning of the British Empire.

The Czar of All Russia

RUSSIA TODAY—the Soviet Union—is the largest nation in the world. It lies half in Europe and half in Asia, and is a mixture of people and ideas from both continents. Until the seventeenth century the eyes and interests of Russia were turned away from Europe. In turn, European courts and kings thought of Russians, "the Muscovites," as barbarians.

Then came a ruler, or *czar*, named Peter. Everything about the young ruler was unusual. He stood 6 feet, 8 inches tall, and could break horseshoes with his bare hands. Peter, who came to be called "the Great," was a

master of war, government, and diplomacy. He was also a fine engineer, sailor, ironsmith—and a good drummer!

Peter looked west to Europe. He was bold, curious, energetic—and tired of his country being thought of as uncivilized. He had a violent temper and a wide streak of cruelty. He was determined to make Russia a modern nation, by force if necessary.

As a young man, Peter studied ships in England, worked with Dutch sailors and ship builders, and brought naval experts back to build up Russia's navy. Peter was the first czar ever to travel outside Russia! When he got home, he looked at the long beards and robes of the Russian nobles and declared they were too old-fashioned

and Asian. With his own hands he snipped off the courtiers' beards. Then he outlawed their traditional way of dressing. Peter himself, though called "Czar of All Russia," usually wore just a simple tunic.

Much of Peter's 43-year reign was spent in waging war, making alliances, and trying to make Russia into a united country. Russia at that time had no "warm water" port. It could trade with the world only when its harbors were not frozen over. Sweden, then Russia's greatest enemy, controlled the Baltic Sea. After almost 20 years of war, Peter defeated Sweden and seized the small countries that kept him from the Baltic seaports. Then he went to war with Turkey, to gain another outlet to the oceans through the Black Sea.

Until Peter the Great, Moscow had been Russia's capital, rich with government buildings, domed cathedrals, and the old fortress called the Kremlin. It was like Peter to build a new capital, pattern it after European cities, and name it after himself.

In 1703 St. Petersburg (the city now called Leningrad) was built on the marshy banks of the Neva river, near Sweden and Finland. A legend among the Finnish people said that St. Petersburg was built in the airy blue sky and lowered to the river banks. It was their way of explaining why the city did not sink into the marsh!

Palaces were built like those Peter had seen in Italy, with elaborate painted plaster decorations. In less than ten years, a thousand nobles and their families moved from Moscow to the new city, as the czar wished. Hundreds of merchants, shopkeepers, and craftsmen followed. Italian, French, Dutch, and German architects worked in the Czar's city.

Many workers were killed in building the city. As in all of Russia then, they were badly paid and badly treated. Some were not paid at all. One noble was shocked that the Czar's Treasury should be expected to pay such people. "There are enough sticks in Russia to thrash those who refuse," he said.

Although he had boundless energy, and the ability to organize the empire, win wars, and bring the learning of Europe into "barbaric" Russia, Peter the Great was not a real reformer. As Russia grew in size and strength, the peasants became poorer. Some were slaves, or *serfs*. Peter was dedicated to a country, but not to its people.

The Little Corporal
Brings Glory to France

NAPOLEON BONAPARTE, like Alexander the Great and Julius Caesar, was a great soldier who rose to command in troubled times. He dreamed of bringing the whole world under one peaceful rule — his own.

Born on the island of Corsica in the Mediterranean Sea, Napoleon went to France to study at a military school. Then he joined the French army. Because he was little more than five feet tall, his fellow officers called him the "Little Corporal."

France at that time was in trouble. The people were poor and starving for bread. The nobles lived in luxury and could not understand the problems of the poor. When Queen Marie Antoinette heard that the people had no bread, all she could think of to say was "Let them eat cake, then!" In 1789 the people started a revolution, and off went the heads of the king and the queen. Many other nobles were executed by the *guillotine*, too.

In the meantime, Napoleon, the Little Corporal, was winning fame by routing the English and Spanish navies at Toulon. Soon Napoleon was named commander in chief of the French army fighting in Italy. There he won battle after battle. Living in Italy, the land of the Caesars, he dreamed of ruling France first, and then the world.

Returning to Paris, the great city of France, Napoleon was hailed as a conqueror.

He decided to invade Egypt next. This would weaken England — France's greatest enemy — by cutting off England's trade with India. Napoleon's navy was badly beaten by the English, but he won against the Egyptians on land.

Within a month after his return to Paris, Napoleon was able to name himself "dictator" of France.

Under Napoleon, France became the leading power of Europe. In 1802, the "Little Corporal" named himself the ruler of France for life.

Now Napoleon began to reorganize his government. He made one set of laws, the *Code Napoleon,* for the whole French nation. Before this, each town and little village had had its own laws. The Code Napoleon freed slaves, guaranteed freedom of worship, and provided equal treatment of all citizens. Public schools were begun.

In 1804, Napoleon had himself crowned Emperor of France. The French nation again had one-man rule, just as it had before the revolution. Slowly, he restored the privileges of the nobles. The court of Napoleon became like the courts of the kings.

The next year, in 1805, Britain organized a number of European countries against France. Napoleon wanted to attack England. He even thought of digging a tunnel under the English Channel, because he knew the English navy was too strong for him to attack by sea. His engineers convinced him, however, that digging such a long tunnel would be too difficult. Since he could not attack

England, Napoleon looked eastward for other countries to conquer.

Napoleon marched across Germany and easily conquered Vienna, the capital of Austria. Then he turned toward Russia, an ally of Austria.

A grand army of 600,000 men under French banners invaded Russia in 1812. The Russians fell back. They burned their fields and cities as they retreated so that the French could not live off the land. In the midst of the bitter Russian winter, the French found themselves masters of nothing, exactly as did the Germans under Hitler more than a century later.

The French were forced to go home. Only 20,000 troops survived the long, terrible march.

The retreat from Russia was the start of a long line of defeats for Napoleon. The armies of several European nations invaded Paris in 1813, and one year later Napoleon gave up his throne. He was exiled to Elba, an island in the Mediterranean.

In 1815 Napoleon came back to France. As the "Little Corporal" marched from the seacoast to Paris, he gathered his old troops together. His people still loved him. The allies, however, won the final victory at Waterloo, in Belgium. Napoleon was captured again.

This time, the British took him farther away from France. They imprisoned him on the barren island of St. Helena, off the coast of Africa.

The "Little Corporal" was born on an island, and came to rule France and conquer most of Europe. He had brought glory to France in a span of less than 25 years. The "Little Corporal" died on an island, exiled from France, but not forgotten.

The Age of Conflict

MUCH OF THE HISTORY of early man, and the rise and fall of empires like those of Persia, Egypt, Rome, Arabia, the Incas, and the British, has been about war. People fighting for land, for food, for rich gold and silver, for sea trade, for strong beliefs.

Wars have changed, too. In the Dark Ages in Europe they had rules of war. Wars could only be fought in warm weather. They were fought in the daytime. They were not fought on Sundays. Every forty days, the armies went home. This is not to say these wars were any less fierce and final than wars are today.

But today things happen faster and faster, in less and less time. New ways of traveling and communicating have brought nations closer and closer together.

After Napoleon, almost a century passed in which European principalities, kingdoms, and city-states became united into nations. Boundary lines were drawn. Sometimes they were fought over.

In 1870, Prussia, the northern part of Germany, invaded and defeated France. It was a short war. That same year was also the beginning of Germany as one nation. The north and south of Germany united under one government and one emperor.

Also in 1870 the many city-states of Italy were drawn together under one king, for the first time since the Roman Empire. In the Orient, Japan warred with China in 1894, and took Korea.

During much of the last 100 years, nations have competed with each other for trade. They competed with each other for control of undeveloped parts of the world, such as Africa, parts of Asia, islands in the oceans. Nations tried to get raw materials such as oil, iron, grain, coal, meat, and metals. Nations looked to find new markets — people to buy the raw materials after they were manufactured into different things. Nations tried to get more land — so that they could expand and colonize and control markets and raw materials.

In 1914, something happened in Europe. In a small country, Serbia, a visiting archduke of Austria was shot. This became important only because it gave Austria a reason to invade Serbia, and so start World War I.

It was called a "World War" because there were many nations fighting together on each side. All the reasons that had united people into nations became forces that set groups of nations against each other.

Germany, Austria and Turkey were united on one side. France, England, Russia and Japan were united on the other side. Italy started on the side of Germany, then changed and joined England.

After four years, during which millions lost their lives, Germany was finally defeated. The United States had tried to remain neutral, but after almost three years it joined with France and England. World War I ended November 11, 1918.

After World War I, Europe was exhausted, but no nation was so completely exhausted as Germany. The ruler of Germany, the Kaiser, was in exile. Germany became a republic, but the democratic way was not to last very long. A world-wide depression made conditions worse in exhausted Europe. A man called Adolf Hitler, who had been an Austrian soldier, began to promise Germany everything.

To all Germans, he promised power as a "master race." He shouted over and over again, "Europe today— the world tomorrow." This was not new. Napoleon had said the same to the French when they had invaded Germany more than a century earlier. To the industrialists, Hitler promised the smashing of trade unions.

To the workers in the unions he promised better wages. To the old nobles, he promised to revive the German Empire and all its old glories.

Meanwhile in Italy, Benito Mussolini was doing much the same thing. He promised a war-weakened, hungry people that they would get food, jobs, and a return to the glories of the Roman Empire.

In the far east, Japan had grown overcrowded. The Japanese wanted land in China and islands in the Pacific. Japan invaded China in 1937.

World War II officially began on September 1, 1939 when Germany invaded Poland. As an ally of Germany, Russia invaded Poland sixteen days later.

Once again, the United States tried to stay neutral. But France fell to Germany, and German planes bombed

London. It looked, this time, as if the promise of Hitler would come true. Germany would rule all Europe — and perhaps the world next. On December 7, 1941, Japan, an ally of Germany, struck at Pearl Harbor, the American naval base in Hawaii. The United States was no longer neutral.

While the United States was fighting Japan in the Pacific, Germany turned on Russia and invaded their former ally's land. Napoleon had made the same mistake more than a century earlier. It is interesting how many times history repeats itself.

Gradually England, Russia, the United States, and their allies worked to victory in Europe. Victory came in the Pacific shortly after the United States dropped the first atomic bomb on Japan, in August, 1945.

At the war's end, the United Nations was formed. The League of Nations which had been formed after World War I had failed to prevent another big war. Perhaps now the United Nations could.

There have been a number of conflicts placed before the United Nations. The war in Korea involved the United Nations, as did the conflicts between Israel and the Arab nations. There have been several conflicts in Africa that have been brought to the United Nations.

The United Nations can be only as strong and as fair as individual members allow it to be. When either side in a dispute refuses to listen to the UN or to abide by its decision, the United Nations has not had the power to force an end to the conflict. So the world still does not live in peace. Russians and Americans engage in a continuous cold war. East and West Berliners are separated by a wall. Israeli and Arab troops remain fully armed despite numerous cease fires. In Indochina, the United States for years was involved in a long, complex battle with Communist forces.

America's Story

A Prince
Sails the Seas

AMERICA'S STORY really begins when people from other parts of the world finally found it between the two greatest oceans. But before that could happen, men had to venture out bravely on these waters.

In the little country of Portugal at the beginning of the fifteenth century a boy named Henry heard tales of the terrors in the ocean. Beyond sight of land, it was said, the water grew so hot that it boiled day and night. Serpents attacked any ship foolish enough to sail on the Sea of Darkness. And even if a man somehow escaped these dangers, something made his skin change color!

When he grew older, Henry was given a chance by his father (who happened to be King of Portugal) to lead a voyage across the sea to the continent of Africa. And Henry did it, even though he was little more than twenty years old.

From that time on, Prince Henry knew what he wanted to do with his life; he would conquer the Sea of Darkness. He had heard of its terrors, but he had also learned something of its ways. Besides, the tales of terror were not the only tales he had heard. He had also heard tales that there were riches beyond the sea to the east.

Many of these stories came from Marco Polo (and his father and uncle), who was the first European to travel through much of the East.

What Marco Polo learned helped to make it possible for men to make maps of a world they had not yet seen.

People knew that one way to the East would be to sail around Africa. But no one knew how large Africa was or for how long a time a ship would have to sail to reach the end of it.

For many years, Prince Henry sent out ships and crews to explore the coast of Africa. He hired specially trained men to teach his captains and pilots all that was known about navigation, astronomy, and map making. His ships were said to be the best of their day.

Prince Henry's crews explored far down the coast of Africa, and some of them brought back gold dust and other treasure. None of them, however, reached the Cape of Good Hope at the tip of Africa.

In 1460 Prince Henry died. He and his crews had failed to reach the Indies by going around Africa. However, he had improved ship building and navigation. He had helped rid men's minds of the fear of the sea. Most important, he had made exploring popular. In the years after his death dozens of men went exploring, following the example of Prince Henry of Portugal.

One Man
Finds America

CHRISTOPHER COLUMBUS, born in Genoa, Italy, in the fifteenth century, first sailed on a ship when he was fourteen.

When he was a young man in his late twenties he had to seek refuge at Lisbon, Portugal, because a ship he had been sailing on was attacked by a pirate ship. It was in Portugal that he met the woman he later married. Her father had been a captain in the service of Prince Henry. It was from his father-in-law's records and from listening to Portuguese sailors that Columbus began to think of a new route to the east. Instead of seeking a sea route east around Africa to the Indies, why not sail *west* to get there? The idea that the world was round was not new. Many educated men of that time believed it.

Columbus presented his plan to the man who was then King of Portugal. Although the King was interested in the idea, he told Columbus he was not—and then secretly he sent others on such a route. But they soon turned back.

Columbus learned about the secret voyage and felt betrayed. He left Portugal and went to Spain. Queen Isabella of Spain had faith in Columbus' idea. If her country could find and control a way to the Indies, the riches of the East would be hers. But Spain was then at war. It was years before the Queen could provide Columbus with the ships and the money that he needed for the voyage.

Early in August of 1492, Columbus finally set sail with three small ships—the *Santa Maria*, the *Pinta*, and the *Nina*—and eighty-eight seamen. According to Columbus, they would reach Japan in a single month.

They sailed westward for over two months, however, and found nothing. The crewmen grew anxious. On the ninth of October, they forced Columbus to agree that if land weren't sighted within three days, he would turn back to Spain.

At two o'clock on the morning of the third day, they saw land!

At dawn Columbus led a party ashore on an island. For three months he explored several islands, looking for the cities of Cathay and the silk-clad merchants described by Marco Polo.

He found only palm huts and people who wore no clothes at all. Still, Columbus believed that these islands were the Indies, and so he called the people *Indians*.

Though Columbus had found no riches, he received a wonderful welcome when he returned to Spain. The King and Queen granted him the title he had demanded, "Admiral of the Ocean."

Columbus made three more trips across the Atlantic, hunting for riches he never found. He died early in the sixteenth century, still believing that Cathay and the passage to India were just beyond the next island.

The exact date of Columbus' birth is not known. In most states, Columbus Day is celebrated on the second Monday in October to commemorate his landing in the New World at a place he named San Salvador.

Two Men Named John

WHEN 144 ENGLISHMEN landed in America in the spring of 1607, one of them was under arrest. He was Captain John Smith. Trouble had broken out aboard ship, and he was blamed.

A company of London merchants had sent them to try their luck in the New World. The merchants paid for the ships and supplies. In return, the settlers were to send back whatever they found of value in Virginia. Gold was what they hoped to find.

When they got to Virginia, the colonists named their settlement Jamestown, for King James of England. And they set Captain Smith free to help build a fort. Soon the men were turning to their former prisoner for advice. It was well they did because these men needed a strong leader, and John Smith was such a man. Many of the settlers were "gentlemen" who had never done an hour's hard work. To make matters worse, the neighboring Indians were far from friendly.

As the summer grew hotter and food grew scarcer, many men became sick and died. By fall only thirty-eight of them were still alive. The settlement seemed doomed to failure. But Smith would not give up. He set out in search of help from . . . the Indians!

But the Indians seized Smith and dragged him before their chief, Powhatan.

The chief ordered that Smith be killed, but Powhatan's young daughter, Pocahontas, pleaded for the Captain's life. The chief gave in. This would have been enough to be grateful for. But Smith found he was luckier than he had thought. He learned that if the Indians spared the life of an enemy, it was their custom to accept him as a friend. So they not only saved his life, but they provided him with the food that the colony needed to keep the rest of the men from starving.

After a time, more men arrived from England. The Indians could not feed them all. The new settlers could have grown corn, but they were much more interested in finding gold. Finally Smith made a rigid rule—any man who would not work would not get food. To some it seemed a hard rule, but it was a necessary one.

Things went better after that, until Captain Smith was hurt in an accident and had to go back to England.

With him gone, the colonists returned to their old ways—and so did the Indians. That winter many men starved in Jamestown.

But the next spring new supplies came from England, and a man named John Rolfe came, too. Instead of wasting time searching for gold, Rolfe grew a plant he saw the Indians using, tobacco. Soon tobacco became popular in Europe. The colonists found they could sell as much of it as they were able to grow. Tobacco proved to be the *real* wealth of Virginia.

Just as important, Rolfe married the Indian princess Pocahontas, and the Indians became good friends with the colonists. Thus America had its first successful colony, thanks to these two men named John—and to an Indian girl, too.

The Pilgrims at Plymouth

THE VERY LAST THING that the Pilgrims expected to find in the American wilderness was an English-speaking Indian! They had not even planned on landing in a wilderness. But they did.

The Pilgrims were also called Puritans, because they wanted the Church of England to reform itself even more than it had done after its separation from the Catholic Church.

So in 1620 they sailed on the ship *Mayflower*, in search of a new land where they would be free to establish the kind of church they wanted. They set out for

Virginia, where a colony had already succeeded. It was a long, stormy crossing.

When at last land was sighted, the Pilgrims found they were far to the north of Virginia. They were at a place that had been explored by Captain John Smith some years before. It was a place he called "Plymouth," in an area he had named "New England."

Should they set sail again? It was winter now. They decided they would have to stay where they were even though there was no one to help them survive in the wilderness.

Before they left the *Mayflower,* the Pilgrims signed one of the most important papers in America's story— the Mayflower Compact. In it they agreed to elect their own leaders and to permit people to vote on the laws that would govern them. This was the first democratic document in the new world.

After they went ashore, the Pilgrims discovered some corn that Indians had buried, and farther on they found a good spot to settle. The land had been cleared but there were no Indians to be seen.

That first winter at Plymouth colony was extremely cold and hard. Many of the Pilgrims died. But spring brought them new hope. It also brought them a new friend. He was an Indian called Squanto—and he spoke English.

Some years before, Squanto had been taken to England by a ship's captain, and he had lived there for ten years. When at last he came home, Squanto found that all of his tribe had died from disease. When he found the Pilgrims living in the same place where his

own people had made their home, he decided to stay with them.

Squanto taught the Pilgrims many things that they needed to know about surviving in this new place. He taught them how to grow corn, how to fish and hunt, how to find and use the strange plants that grew there. And he helped them to make friends and live in peace with the other Indians in the area.

The Pilgrims worked very hard. When autumn came, they had large stores of food for the winter ahead. So they held a special feast to thank God for all the help that they had received—and they asked the Indians to join them. This was the first "Thanksgiving."

News of Plymouth reached other Puritans across the ocean, and they decided to attempt the long journey to America. These people also wanted to be free to worship and to live as they saw fit. Just as important, they also had the same willingness to work.

They, too, landed near Plymouth, and one day the colonists of Plymouth and the newer and larger colony all united. They formed the Massachusetts Bay colony, one of the largest and most important of the early American colonies.

Colonial Life

A PERSON HAD TO HAVE a strong body and an alert mind to stay alive in early America. Houses, furniture, clothing and the tools to shape them all had to be made by hand.

In the very beginning, the colonists had no houses at all—just holes dug out of hillsides and covered over with branches and bark cut from the trees. Their only heat came from open fires, where the women also cooked.

Just as soon as they could, the colonists began cutting down trees to build houses. Each house had only a single room. Sometimes there was also a small balcony overhead, where things could be stored. The older children usually slept on the balcony, too.

Nails were few, so houses and furniture were held together with wooden pegs. For beds the colonists strung ropes between wooden frames to hold mattresses often stuffed with corn husks. In winter, the settlers covered themselves with another one of these mattresses to keep warm. They ate from wooden plates with wooden spoons.

A huge fireplace was built along one wall. The ashes from the fireplace were never thrown away, but were carefully saved in a large barrel. They were soaked in water, and lye was made from them. Women mixed the lye with melted fat from animals and boiled it all in big kettles to make soap!

The women also hung a number of pieces of string from a stick and dipped them in melted fat, then lifted them out and let the fat harden. Then they would dip them again and again. Each time the strings would pick up a little more fat until, after many, many dippings, they became candles.

Every home had its own garden, where the settlers grew vegetables. The houses were usually built around a meadow, which was called the "common" because it was for everyone's use. Here the animals grazed.

Outside the village, in large fields, they planted corn. Every day except Sunday, the men trudged to work there. On Sunday they went to church, both in the morning and the afternoon.

Doing everything for themselves did not make for an easy life, but it was worth the hardships to America's early settlers. Now they had the freedom that they valued so highly and, as time went on, they had better houses and more comforts. Blacksmiths came to make iron tools instead of wooden ones. Glassmakers, carpenters, and skilled workmen of all kinds soon began to appear. After a while, one community was trading with another for the things that it needed.

The colonists became very proud of the life that they had made in a new world, and proudest of all that they were free to govern themselves.

Ben Franklin
Writes to His Friends

BY THE TIME A MAN named Benjamin Franklin became a famous American, America had changed quite a lot since the days of the first settlers.

The number of colonies had grown to thirteen, and naturally there were many more people. Ben himself came from a family of nineteen. Many of this growing number of Americans were dissatisfied with the way the King of England was treating America.

The Americans no longer had many of the freedoms they used to have. The King made laws for them, instead of letting people vote. He made them pay heavy taxes and did not let them have anything to say about how the money would be spent.

Franklin was an adventurous man of great energy and sparkling humor. He had gained fame as a printer, an inventor, a scientist, and a number of other things. He was a very wise and peaceful man. He went to England to try to settle the differences between England and the colonies. He hoped that England would return some freedom to the colonies and that the colonies would remain loyal to England. Yet no matter what Ben Franklin said, the King of England stubbornly refused to listen.

Finally, even the peace-loving Franklin saw that only actions—not words—would return freedom to the colonies. He began writing letters to important people in each of the colonies, telling them what was going on and what might be best done about it. In turn, those men wrote to others, so that soon all the American leaders throughout the colonies knew the same facts and were of the same mood.

Through these Committees of Correspondence, as the letter writers came to be known, the colonists began to think of themselves more as American citizens than as British citizens. They began to have a unity that they had never had before. This spirit of American unity prepared the way for the coming revolution. Benjamin Franklin, the famed peacemaker, had become Ben Franklin, the American patriot.

Guns Begin to Boom

THE BOAT BRINGING Benjamin Franklin back to America was still at sea when the first shots were fired between the English and Americans.

On the night of April 18, 1775, the British general in Boston ordered his troops to seize some guns and gunpowder that the Americans were hiding in the nearby town of Concord.

But as soon as the soldiers left for Concord, someone signaled with a lantern. A man named Paul Revere leaped on his horse and rode through the night to give warning that the English were on their way.

By the next morning the British troops had reached
Lexington, a town close to Concord. And several dozen
Americans, called "Minutemen"—because they were
ready to take up arms against the English at just a minute's notice—were waiting for them.

"Don't fire unless fired upon," their leader said. "But if they want a war . . . let it begin here."

And it began there. The British fired, killing eight Americans and wounding ten more. Then they marched toward Concord. But the Americans had had time to hide their supply of guns and gunpowder, and the British found little there. Then Minutemen poured into Concord from all over the countryside and drove the British back. Minutemen fired at the British from behind fences and trees all along the road to Boston. The Americans lost almost 100 men that day, but the British lost three times that many.

The Southern colonists were just as ready to fight for *their* liberties as were New England's Minutemen. The Virginians, too, had a store of gunpowder. The day after the fighting at Lexington and Concord, the royal governor of Virginia ordered his men to seize the gunpowder stored at Williamsburg. Americans with guns stood up to the British and would not let them take the powder, and the British chose not to answer with force.

But in Boston the fighting grew more bitter. The Americans made a stand on Breed's Hill. They knew that if they could hold the high places above Boston Harbor, they could sink the English ships in the harbor.

The British charged up the hill. They were driven back once, then again. But finally they took it, along with nearby Bunker Hill. The victory cost the British over a thousand men—a loss "greater than we can bear," as their general wrote home.

There was another hill above the harbor—Dorchester Heights. But the British knew the Americans had no cannon to put up there, so they did not bother with it. This turned out to be a bad decision.

Two weeks later, a rich farmer and soldier from Virginia, George Washington, arrived and took command of the American troops. While Washington worked to build a real army, other help was on the way. Americans dragged 60 cannons into Boston and set them up on Dorchester Heights.

When these cannons were aimed at the harbor, the British ships were forced to pull out. A year after Lexington, the British had lost all of New England. The colonies were not yet independent, but they had let the British know they knew how to fight.

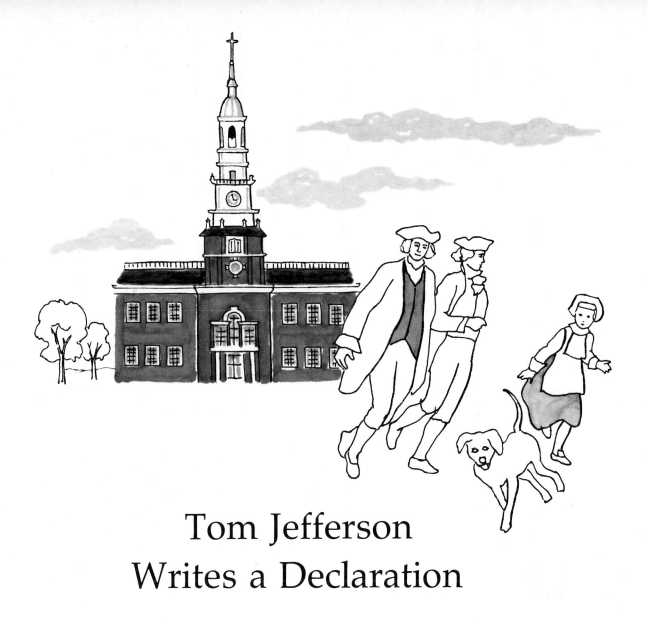

Tom Jefferson
Writes a Declaration

THREE MONTHS AFTER the English were driven from Boston, each of the colonies sent men to an important meeting in Philadelphia, called the Continental Congress.

Most of the members of the Congress had decided that the time had come to break all ties with England. A few members still hoped that the King of England could be persuaded to give in to the colonies' demands for more freedom. Some others were afraid of England's power. After much debate, the Congress appointed a committee to write a paper saying that the American

colonies were no longer part of the British Empire, but were "free and independent states."

One of the members of the committee was a young man from Virginia, Thomas Jefferson. Like his friend Patrick Henry, Tom Jefferson was a lawyer. Like George Washington, he was a rich farmer. Like Ben Franklin, he was an inventor. Best of all, he was an excellent writer. So the others asked him to write this important paper.

Thomas Jefferson did the job so well that his "Declaration of Independence" has been a model for every free country ever since. He began by saying that "all men are created equal," and that they have the right to "life, liberty, and the pursuit of happiness." And when any government tries to take away these rights, Jefferson went on, the people have the right to overthrow that government and set up a new one.

John Adams and Franklin made just a few small changes in this important declaration. Then they took it to the members of the Congress for approval.

The Congress made one very important change in the Declaration. Jefferson wrote that the King had made the colonies buy slaves, and that now the states would end slavery. But a great number of people from the South did not want to lose their slaves. They were backed by certain men from the North who made money by bringing the slaves in ships from Africa.

So Jefferson could not end slavery. Still, the rest of the Declaration of Independence was approved by the Congress, and on July 4, 1776, it was signed by men from every part of America.

The thirteen colonies had now *declared* their independence. But now they would have to fight a great war to make it come true.

George Washington Tricks the British

BEFORE THE REVOLUTIONARY War began there were many Americans who were willing to fight against England for their freedom. There were others who feared that England was too big and too strong for the colonies to fight against. There were even some who were still loyal to England.

Even after the Revolutionary War began, there were many who feared that the colonies were making a mistake. The American soldiers had little training, but the British soldiers were very well trained. The British troops had better uniforms and better equipment. Many colo-

124

nists felt that America was likely to lose the war and that then the new country would be worse off than it had been when they were just thirteen colonies.

After a few early victories, things went badly for the Americans. The British forced George Washington's troops from New York City. Then they chased the American soldiers through New Jersey and across the Delaware river into Pennsylvania.

The British general, Cornwallis, thought the Americans were beaten. He wrote back to England that the war would be over soon.

George Washington knew that something had to be done. He had to prove to his soldiers, to the Congress, and to the American people that his ragged American troops could beat the British. If his troops felt they could not win, they would leave the Army and go home. Congress would refuse to vote more money for the war. The American people would give up the effort to be free.

A long winter was coming when little fighting could be done. Washington knew that food would be scarce and that many times his soldiers would go hungry. Their clothing was poor and he knew they would suffer from the cold. He wanted his soldiers and the American people to have a shining memory of victory to carry them through the bitter winter months.

Washington put into action a daring plan. In a heavy snowstorm on Christmas night, in 1776, Washington led his troops back across the Delaware River and attacked the British forces at Trenton. He divided his soldiers in two sections. One group attacked from the south and the other from the north. Together, they caught the enemy in between. In less than one hour, Washington had killed or captured every one of them!

When Cornwallis got news of this, he hurried from New York to attack the Americans. But Washington, knowing that he had done the important thing that he had set out to do, fooled the British general and led his troops away in the dark of night.

The next morning, while Cornwallis was wondering where the American soldiers had gone, Washington attacked the British at nearby Princeton and won still another victory!

Washington's soldiers spent the rest of the freezing winter at Valley Forge. They had no money at all to buy food, clothes, or other supplies. Many of them went barefoot in the biting snow. But one thing carried them through—they now knew they could beat the British. Washington's "trick" at Trenton had given them the will to fight on and to win.

And win they did. On October 19, 1781, Cornwallis surrendered his army to George Washington. The war was over, and now the Americans had truly won their independence.

ARTICLES OF Confederation AND Perpetual Union BETWEEN THE

Making a Nation

IN ITS OWN WAY, making the thirteen separate states into a single nation was a harder job than winning the war. For, although they *called* themselves "united," the truth was that each state went its own way.

While they were still battling the British, all the states had signed what were called Articles of Confederation. This document gave the Continental Congress the authority to fight the war. But it did not give Congress the power to collect taxes, to make laws, or to settle quarrels between the states. And soon the states did begin quarreling among themselves.

Some men began to see that what was needed was a strong government with the power to make the states work together. A convention was called to create a new system, a plan "to form a more perfect union." George Washington, the hero of the Revolution, was asked to take charge of the project.

A great deal of discussion went into the writing of a new Constitution, the one we still have today. More work was needed to persuade the states to accept this list of important "rules" for the new country.

Yet the Constitution still was really only something written on paper. Whether it worked depended on the living men who ran the government.

In 1789, George Washington became the first President of the United States. His Secretary of the Treasury, Alexander Hamilton, suggested that the United States government should pay the debts of the individual states for the cost of the Revolutionary War. The states saw that they had more to gain than to lose by obeying the federal government. Now the European countries across the ocean could no longer look upon the United States as a poor country that could not even pay its debts.

The government could raise the money it needed by collecting taxes. But some people who made whiskey in Pennsylvania refused to pay a tax on whiskey. Knowing that the laws had to be respected by all the citizens, President Washington quickly dealt with this "Whiskey Rebellion." He sent troops to Pennsylvania at once. He wanted to let everyone know that the government of the United States was able and ready to make sure its laws were obeyed.

John Adams, the second President, showed that the United States would stand firm when threatened by a foreign country, France. Thomas Jefferson, the third President, bought from France a huge amount of land west of the Mississippi River. This land became known as the Louisiana Purchase, but much more than the present state of Louisiana was included. The United States had doubled its size.

Jefferson sent two frontiersmen, Meriwether Lewis and William Clark, to explore this new territory. They sent back good news, saying that it was a beautiful area.

Soon wagons were rolling toward the West, carrying settlers to these new lands. The new nation had proved it had the strength to survive. Now it was growing bigger and bigger.

Johnny Appleseed
Walks West

WHEN SETTLERS MOVED westward into the states
of Ohio and Indiana and Illinois, many of them met a
mystery.

Only Indians had ever lived there before, yet in
place after place they found apple trees growing in neat
rows! Sturdy fences protected the trees from hungry
animals. They wondered who could have planted apple
trees and built the fences.

News about it spread from cabin to cabin. Finally
people discovered that there was a stranger walking
alone through the wilderness ahead, with a cooking pot

130

on his head and a great sack slung over his shoulder. In the sack were countless apple seeds, and whenever he came upon a place that seemed a good spot for people to live, he paused and planted a few seeds. He was named John Chapman, but people naturally came to call him Johnny Appleseed.

Born in Massachusetts, Johnny was a very religious boy who had a special feeling about apples. When he was quite young, Johnny vowed that he would travel to the lands where people were just beginning to settle. There, he would share with them the joys of his religion, and he would "comfort" them "with apples," as the words from the Bible go.

Wherever he went, this amazing man put apple seeds into the earth, so that apples would be waiting for the new settlers when they arrived. If he met people along the way, he gave young apple trees and seeds to them. As the years went by, he traveled back to the many places where he had planted his trees to take care of them. More than anything else, he wanted people to have sweet, healthy apples to eat, and bright pink apple blossoms to see every spring.

Once in a while, he traded his trees for food to eat, or even sold them for the little money that he needed to live. But most of the time he simply gave trees away. As time passed, just about everyone knew Johnny Appleseed and was very glad to see him.

People liked to listen to his stories even more than they loved his apples. Johnny gave them news of other settlers—like the seven members of the Ross family who all lived for many months in a hollow tree! He also told them that some Indians had tried to kill him once, and how he had gotten away from them by jumping into a pond and hiding under the muddy water for a long time. He did it by breathing through a hollow reed that he had found growing on the water's edge. It was a trick Johnny had learned from the Indians a long time ago!

For the Indians almost never bothered Johnny Appleseed. To them he was very strange, but harmless. They knew that he never carried a gun, because it was part of his creed not to take a life—man or animal. Johnny never ate meat from the time he was a child.

Johnny always was free to come and go as he pleased—and that meant that he was able to warn settlers when Indians were about to attack them. When the Indians and the settlers were at peace again, Johnny Appleseed wandered on, planting more seeds in the ground of America's untraveled territory.

Frontier Life

THE PEOPLE WHO OPENED UP the West hoped to find a better life. The East had become crowded, and had more people than there were jobs to offer them.

People came in wagons and on horseback. A few of them, like John James Audubon, even floated down the Ohio River in flat-bottomed boats. Later Audubon became famous the world over for his paintings of the birds he saw in the forests and fields of America.

The first real pioneers were woodsmen, who lived where none but Indians had ever been before. Most often they were not married, though a few had wives and families. A man would start by cutting down some trees in order to put up a rough cabin, and where the trees had been he would plant some corn. Most of his time he spent in the woods hunting.

The true farmers came after the woodsmen. A lot of them were really not very good at what they did, and they had to try very hard to make a go of it. Their cabins were better than the woodsmen's, though, and of course they planted more crops.

Some farmers had help in building their cabins. Because they were all in the wilderness together, the pioneers on the frontier were glad to help one another. After a man had cut enough logs, his "neighbors" would

come from many miles away to help him build a cabin. Once the cabin was up, they next made a rough bench and table to work and eat on, and a platform on which to sleep. There usually was no other furniture in the house.

A frontiersman usually had some horses and a cow. He fed them by turning them loose in the nearby woods where they found their own food. Too often there was not much food to find, so the cow gave little milk and the horses were too weak for heavy work. When the cow gave milk, there was no way to keep it cool, and it quickly turned sour. But the pioneers didn't let that bother them. They claimed sour milk tasted better.

Indians were a threat every day of the year. A frontier family had to be prepared at all times to rush to the nearest fort when they were near enough to hear a neighbor give the alarm. When they weren't that fortunate, they had to be ready to fight. There was simply no

way to escape a life on the frontier that was even harder than life in the colonies had been. Often the frontier farmer finally had to sell everything and move on, in order to pay what he owed.

The farmer who succeeded was often the man who was able to buy good tools and strong, healthy animals. Usually he was the man who came from the East with a little money, and bought the land from the very first pioneers. With good tools he grew more crops, and even had time to plant a vegetable garden. His barn was often much nicer than his own house, since animals which were kept warm needed less food and stayed healthier.

He drank sour milk too, but he had enough of it to make butter and cheese as well. After a while, he had enough animals to give meat to his family. That meant he saved the time of going into the woods to hunt for it. He kept the meat from spoiling by cutting it into strips and hanging them in front of the fire to dry.

When it was ready, the meat was called *jerky*, and it was hard and tough. But the farmer's wife cooked it in a stew until it finally became tender. Anyone entering a pioneer's house would almost always see a stew pot hung over the fire. As the frontier farmer and his family ate their meals in the warmth of their homes, the woodsmen were pushing on somewhere into a new wilderness.

Andy Jackson
Goes East

MARCH 4, 1829, WAS THE greatest day of all for the people of the new Western frontier. That was the date that Andrew Jackson, a frontiersman just like themselves, moved East—to become the seventh President of the United States!

Before this time, all of the presidents of the country had been wealthy men from Virginia or members of Boston's powerful Adams family. Andy Jackson was very different. He had been born in a cabin in the South Carolina backwoods. His father had died before he was born, and the family was poor as could be.

Andy was wild as a boy, with a temper more fiery than his red hair. He was always getting into fights with bigger boys. He loved fighting. He even fought in the American Revolution, when he was thirteen years old!

Andy lost his family during the war. Without anyone to depend on, Andy Jackson learned to depend upon himself. He became everything from a planter and merchant to a famous Indian fighter, but he didn't learn to read or write until his wife taught him when he was in his twenties! People called him "Old Hickory," because they said a steely hickory nut was the only thing that had the toughness of Andrew Jackson!

"Old Hickory" became a hero of all the West. And it must have seemed as though every person in the West was trying to squeeze into the White House when Andy took office as President.

Men in homespun clothes and coonskin caps had streamed into Washington from every part of the West to cheer their hero. They formed a huge crowd about the White House, where a huge inauguration party was to be held. Andy had said that everyone was invited.

The crowd filling the street was so eager to see Jackson that the guards weren't able to hold them back. People burst through the doors of the White House, smashed plates, and stood on chairs in their muddy boots to get a look at their leader. A happy riot took place. Waiters hauled tubs of punch out to the White House lawns to lure the crowds outside. Washington had never seen anything like this, and never would again!

This incident made the Chief Justice of the Supreme Court say, "The wild asses of the West, led by Andy Jackson, will ruin the government." But Andy Jackson did not ruin the government. During his eight years as President he proved that a common man could not only fight Indians, but run one of the greatest countries in the world, and run it well.

Figure 2

Figure 3

Robert Fulton
Builds a Boat

ONE AUGUST NIGHT, while the United States was still a very young country, hoofbeats were heard through the scattered villages of the Hudson Valley of New York. Fearful voices shouted warnings to sleeping farmers— "The Devil's on his way up the river—in a sawmill!"

Men and women crept to the edge of the water and peered at a strange shape coming up the river—fast— *against* the current. Fire and sparks flew from it into the sky. The bright light from a blazing fire lit up a large wheel with paddles, much like the kind of wheel that turned a sawmill.

No one could go back to sleep after seeing such a sight. The next morning, when they learned what they had really seen, they would not believe it. For it was said to be a boat, powered not by wind—but by steam!

The fire on this amazing boat heated a huge boiler filled with water. When the water turned to steam, the force of the steam turned a large wheel. Paddles on the wheel pushed against the water of the river and made the boat move. A "crazy" man named Robert Fulton had built it.

This was not the first time that Fulton had been called crazy. A lot of people had thought he wasn't quite right in the head for trying to build a steamboat. But Fulton had believed it could be done.

Robert Livingston, the wealthy American Ambassador to France, finally helped Fulton to make his dream come true—for it took money to build a steamboat.

But it was worth it. The steamboat worked! Fulton then began work on a much larger one, called the *Clermont*, after Livingston's home in America.

Even though Fulton had already proved he could do it, almost everyone still laughed at the *Clermont* as soon as they heard of it. They gave it another name— "Fulton's Folly."

Some sailors were afraid that it just might work, however. If it did, they would one day be out of their jobs. So they tried to damage the *Clermont* before it was finished. Fulton had to hire a watchman so that no one would harm his project.

Finally he finished the *Clermont*. Livingston came aboard on August 17, 1807, with a group of relatives and friends—who were all terrified of it.

The *Clermont* started. It moved . . . first slowly, then more quickly . . . onto the river.

Suddenly cheers began coming from the shore. They grew louder and louder. And as the boat began to smoothly cover the miles to Albany, the passengers themselves burst into song. This was surely no "folly."

Fulton was the first man to make a commercially successful steamboat. Soon steamboats were puffing up most of America's big rivers, and steamships were crossing the world's wide oceans.

Steamboats
on the Mississippi

IT WAS A WONDERFUL THING when Robert Fulton invented the steamboat. But a question still remained—how could steamboats sail on the great Mississippi River of America? In the Mississippi, dangerous rocks were always lurking beneath the surface, and sandbars where the boat could run aground were constantly shifting.

But Fulton thought it could be done, and in 1811 he sent Nicholas Roosevelt to try it.

Fulton's friend went to Pittsburgh to oversee the building of the steamboat *New Orleans*. In spite of rapids, floods, and even an earthquake, Roosevelt finally piloted

143

the boat down the Ohio River to the Mississippi and finally all the way to New Orleans. Later a man named Shreve built an improved model that made the trip even faster. Steamboats had come to the Mississippi to stay.

As years passed, the steamboats became larger and more comfortable until they were called "floating palaces." Beautiful furniture and drapes decorated their shining cabins and plush dining rooms.

The "steamers" bought wood from men along the banks of the river, as fuel for the boilers. Woodcutters always kept piles of timber ready, and in the dark of night they would keep a fire going so that the captains of the steamers could always see them. Often if a man could not afford his ticket on a steamboat, he was allowed

to pay his way by helping to get the wood aboard and to stack it on deck close to the boilers.

Races between steamboats soon became a popular sport. People would gather on the high river banks to cheer their favorite. Newspapers printed the results.

Now that the steamer had come to the Mississippi, it no longer took merchants and planters many months to float their goods down to New Orleans on flatboats.

Soon there were hundreds of steamers on the Mississippi moving goods and people to and from New Orleans.

One of the biggest cargoes the steamboats carried was cotton. Cotton planters cleared more and more land in order to plant more cotton, and sent it down to New Orleans where it was shipped out all over the world. They bought more slaves to do the clearing, planting, and picking. Before long these cotton plantations were spread along both sides of the Mississippi.

The cotton that went to England and other places was made into cloth. In return for it, other goods were sent back to America and carried up the river by steamboats to the owners of the plantations.

It took a great war between the South and the North to finally end the wonderful days of the Mississippi steamboats. By that time steam was pulling railroad trains from one end of the nation to the other—much more safely and quickly than the steamboats could travel.

Samuel Morse's
Magic Messages

IN 1832, A FAMOUS PAINTER, Samuel Morse, was
returning to America from a trip to Europe. While he
had been traveling in Europe, Morse had wished that
there were a faster way of hearing from his family back
home in Boston.

One night, while eating dinner on the ship bringing
him home, Morse got talking to some men about electricity. They discussed Ampere, the Frenchman who experi-
mented with electricity, and Ben Franklin, who had
found that electricity flashed through a wire instantly—
no matter how long the wire might be.

147

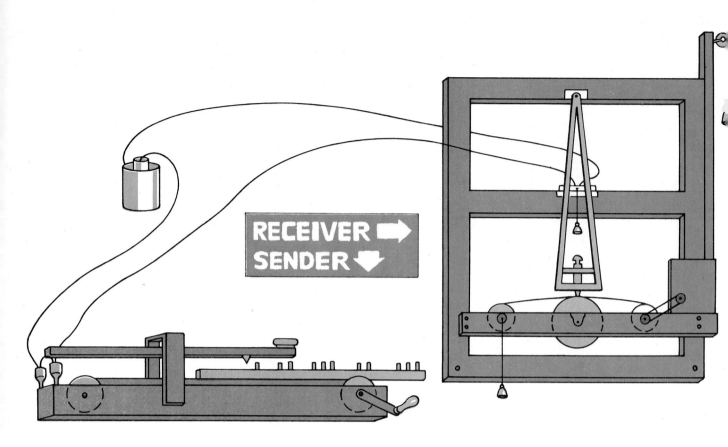

Suddenly an idea flashed through the painter's mind quicker than an electric current. He saw how electricity could send messages from one end of a wire to another—even if the wire stretched between two cities!

Morse went off by himself and tried to figure out every detail of his new idea. First, he would make batteries to produce the electricity. Next, by pressing down on a "key" he could send the electricity through the wire in a group of long and then short bursts. By putting these long and short bursts—or dots and dashes, as he called them—into patterns, he could make a "code" for each letter of the alphabet.

In other words, he could "spell out" a message with long and short bursts of electrical current, and someone miles away at the other end of the wire would get the message right away—and understand it only a few seconds later!

The minute the ship docked in New York, Samuel Morse began work on his invention. Finally, it was done—and he called it the *telegraph*, from two Greek words which meant "to write far."

But, as with all men who do something new and different, Morse had to solve still another problem with his invention—he had to convince people it would work. To prove that, he put rubber around a wire and ran it beneath the water from New York City to an island nearby. A huge crowd gathered to see if the telegraph really could do what Morse claimed.

But it did nothing at all.

Morse soon found out why. A ship had gotten tangled with the wire and the captain had cut it, figuring that it was a fisherman's line!

What hath God

wrought

It wasn't until May of 1844 that Samuel Morse could get the money from the government to test his telegraph again. He strung more than three dozen miles of wire from poles between Baltimore and Washington. Then, with a group of very important people gathered around him in Washington, Morse tapped out the first message ever sent over an outdoor telegraph line.

That message was "invented" by a young woman, who handed it to him in plain sight of everyone there. His partner in Baltimore could not possibly know the message before Morse tapped it out. The message was, "What hath God wrought?"

Almost before the crowd could take a breath, a message flashed back from Baltimore—W...H...A...T... H...A...T...H...G...O...D...W...R...O...U...G...H...T...?

Samuel Morse had "wrought" a "miracle" of communication. Other men later learned to send messages without wires, and even to send pictures through space, but Samuel Morse's telegraph was one of the most exciting and important inventions of his time.

Abe Lincoln
Saves the Union

THE TELEGRAPH WIRES FLASHED a message to a tall man in Springfield, Illinois, on a November night in 1860. The man was Abraham Lincoln, and the message the telegraph brought was that he had been elected President of the United States.

This man who had been born in a log cabin in the state of Kentucky had taken the reins of his country at its turning point.

America was being torn in two over slavery. Because people continued moving West, many more states had been made part of the Union. Most persons in the North felt slavery to be wrong, and did not want it allowed in the new frontier states.

The people in the South violently disagreed. Slavery was the foundation for the way they made their living. The argument grew more bitter, until finally the South threatened to *secede,* or pull out of the United States, unless slavery was permitted everywhere.

Lincoln made a number of speeches against slavery and when he was elected President, the South was outraged. The state of South Carolina seceded. Other Southern states soon did the same. They began their own government as the "Confederate States of America," electing Mississippi's Jefferson Davis as President.

Abe Lincoln had only been in Washington a single month when these Confederate forces started firing on Fort Sumter, a federal fort in South Carolina. Lincoln called for troops. The Civil War had begun.

Though Lincoln had been brought up on a back-woods farm, like Andrew Jackson, he had taught himself many things and had gained a great deal of wisdom. He knew that the South's secession could destroy the Union. He cared about getting rid of slavery, but by far the most important matter to Lincoln was making the Union whole again. So he called up troops to fight. He meant to hold the Southern states in the Union.

In 1863 Lincoln issued the Emancipation Proclamation, declaring that all slaves in Confederate-held territory were freed. For the proclamation to mean anything, the war between North and South first had to be won, however. This took almost three more years.

But finally, the North won and the United States was whole again. President Lincoln had saved the Union.

Mathew Brady
Photographs a War

WHEN THE SOUTHERN SOLDIERS fired on Fort
Sumter, the hoop-skirted women of Charleston went out
on the rooftops and smilingly waved their handkerchiefs
at the men who were starting America's most bitter war.
To them it was the War of Secession, though the North
called it the Civil War.

Just about all the Southerners thought that they
had a right to withdraw from the Union. Moreover, they
expected not only an easy victory, but a short war, too.

Some people in the North also felt that winning
would be quick and simple. When Northern forces first

154

marched to attack the Southerners at Bull Run near Washington, people actually rode out with picnic baskets to watch the battle!

In the Northern cities, men coming home from the battlefields sometimes brought photos with them. Many of the best ones were taken by photographer Mathew Brady. It was Brady who helped the North to understand what a serious thing this war was, and he also helped the North to win it.

For example, in 1862, at the battle of Antietam, Brady's specially built photographic wagon was riddled by bullets. Part of his equipment was destroyed. One of his assistants, Tim O'Sullivan, had a camera shot right out of his hands!

But Brady and his crew never ran from the midst of battle, where they had to be to take their photographs. They fully recorded the horrible battle, in which over 100,000 men fought for fourteen hours without stopping.

Brady captured for all time the explosive fire of the hundreds of cannons and the brutal loss of countless lives. Those pictures went back to his gallery in Washington, but they also went up North for thousands of people to see. When people did see them, they no longer thought of the war as something that would be short or easy.

Brady had shown even greater courage than one might imagine, for in those days over a minute was needed to take a picture! Those sixty seconds could be a lifetime—and on many, many occasions they almost were Brady's lifetime—when bullets and cannon shots were whizzing by. Moreover, Brady could not retreat

to safety even after the picture was taken, for it had to be developed at once.

Mathew Brady was lucky to survive Antietam. Many men did not. He was also fortunate to come out alive from the many other battles of the Civil War that he photographed.

At first, the Union officers felt that Brady was in their way. But at battles like Antietam they saw how his photos might help them win the Civil War!

Through studying every detail of enemy lines in Brady's pictures, the Northern officers could figure out how many guns the enemy had and where they were.

The Northern officers allowed Brady to stay with the army and keep all the money from selling his pictures— if he first took free pictures for them so that they could plan their battles. From that time on Brady went just about everywhere that the Union soldiers did, and he had teams of photographers at other places.

As time passed, he began photographing more and more Northern victories. And Mathew Brady cheered with the Union soldiers when news finally came that on the very same day General Lee was beaten at Gettysburg, General Grant had won an important victory at Vicksburg, Mississippi. Later, Brady was with Grant himself as Union troops took the Confederate capital of Richmond. A week after that, Lee surrendered to Grant.

Four awful years had gone by since Charleston's ladies had cheered the war's beginning. More than half a million men had been wounded or killed. The South was in ruins and would take a long time to recover.

Seven thousand pictures of the Civil War had been taken by Mathew Brady. Some had helped to win it.

Wilbur and Orville
Learn to Fly

SOARING ALL ALONE over the sand dunes, he saw the earth rushing toward him and knew that in a second he would crash.

Wilbur Wright and his glider without an engine were together in the sand when brother Orville ran up. The glider was wrecked, but Wilbur was happy. He wasn't hurt and had accomplished his goal; he had made the glider go up and down—before it crashed.

The Civil War had ended only a few years before Wilbur and Orville Wright were born in Dayton, Ohio. When they were young men, they opened a bicycle shop.

Back of their store was a shed where they did work that would change the world. There they designed and built gliders—planes that soared on the wind.

Wilbur and Orville had read everything that they could find about gliders. They came to realize that all a glider could ever be was a toy—though a very dangerous one—unless it had better power than the on-again, off-again wind. An engine was the answer. But before tackling that problem, the Wright brothers had to figure out a way to raise and lower the glider, as well as make it turn once it was in the air.

So they sent all the pieces of a glider to a lonely place called Kitty Hawk in North Carolina. There they could have a lot of wind to work with and no trees or buildings to get in the way. There would also be no people to laugh at them.

In Kitty Hawk, Wilbur and Orville put their glider together and launched it into the wind. It only bumped along in the air a short distance—but it did fly. They kept trying, changing this or that a little bit with each new attempt. And finally they controlled the glider while it was off the ground! It was the first time this had ever been done.

Wilbur and Orville went home to build a bigger glider with better controls. Then they took it back to Kitty Hawk and, by taking turns flying it again and again, they learned how to steer it. Now they were ready to try powering it with an engine.

A man named Henry Ford was making machines that worked with gasoline engines. People called them "horseless carriages," but later that name would change

to *automobiles*. But Ford's gas engines weighed far too much for a glider. The Wright boys would have to make their own engine.

It was hard to make an engine that would weigh little and still be powerful. Wilbur and Orville worked and worked at it until they thought they had succeeded. But of course they couldn't be sure that the engine would work without trying it.

On December 17, 1903, they flipped a coin to see who would be the first to try it. Orville won. He got into the machine. The time was 10:35 in the morning.

Although the Wright brothers had invited the whole town of Kitty Hawk to watch the great event, almost no one was there. People did not think this would be an event to remember. The Wright brothers barely had any witnesses at all to what they were about to do.

Orville started the engine. The flying machine moved forward, then up, up, up against a strong wind blowing across the sand dunes.

The plane was up—but now how far would it go forward? With Orville lying in his place on the lower wing, the craft began traveling forward.

161

The engine kept barking and the propellers whirling—and the plane traveled a whole hundred feet before Orville took it down!

Then Wilbur got in, opened the throttle, and flew nearly twice as far. On his second try, Wilbur went almost a thousand feet and was in the air for nearly a minute!

Man had flown!

Before too many years had gone by, the Wrights and other men made the airplane better and better until it was taking people over oceans and across continents in just a few hours. The world of Prince Henry and Columbus—even of Robert Fulton and Samuel Morse—had become a much smaller place because of two brothers who wouldn't give up.

A Soldier and a Statesman for Peace

A soldier crept up a hill in France as hundreds of bullets whizzed by him. He saw the German machine guns firing on American troops on top of another hill. Corporal Alvin York had made up his mind to stop those machine guns. He did not like killing, but because his country had been forced into war with Germany, he wanted to help the United States win.

Not long after the Wright brothers made the first successful flight in North Carolina, the German Kaiser, or emperor, began to take control of all Europe. He even wanted to conquer the United States. But soon, twenty-three nations from all over the world joined together against Germany. Calling themselves the "Allies," they turned their battle in Europe into the First World War.

When the Kaiser sank many American ships, the United States was forced to join the Allies. Then, more than two million American soldiers were battling in Europe. That is why, on an October morning in 1918, Alvin York happened to be on a hillside in France.

When this soldier from Tennessee returned to the American lines, he had 132 German prisoners with him. He had killed more than two dozen of the enemy and captured three dozen machine guns. For his heroic deeds he was awarded his country's highest medals of bravery—a whole world cheered him.

While everyone dreamed of an end to the World War, a statesman named Woodrow Wilson dared to think of an end to *all* wars. His vision was even more far-reaching than that of Columbus or the Wright brothers. As President of the United States, he asked Americans to join the Allies for a curious reason—"peace without victory."

Wilson felt that the Allies could win the great war, but still "lose the peace" if they did not work together after the war. He felt we must also become friends with the enemy to keep peace in the world.

When the World War ended, the Allies met in Paris, France to decide on a peace treaty and how to deal with Germany. There, Wilson told the other Allies about his dream for world peace, and how it could come true. Wilson felt that the way to stop any nation from doing what Germany had done was for all nations to meet together in a League of Nations. Every country would be equal; a small country would no longer have to fear a larger one.

The other men in Paris agreed to the League of Nations, but they also insisted that Germany be punished for bringing on the World War. Although this was not quite what Wilson wanted, he had to agree to it. Now, the United States Senate had to agree to the peace treaty and to the League, which had been worked out by the Allies in Paris.

When he came back home to the United States, Wilson found that Americans were against the League of Nations idea because they were afraid of losing their independence. So, the U.S. Senate voted against it, and Woodrow Wilson never saw his dream come true.

Still, Wilson was the first man to inspire people from nations everywhere with the idea of world peace, and that hope has grown over the years. Today, the United Nations is working together as a world peace organization. But, just like the Wright brothers' many attempts to fly an airplane, much work will have to be done before final success comes.

"Lucky" Lindy

TWO WHOLE DAYS and one very stormy night passed while a world sat next to its radios, waiting for news of a young man flying all by himself over the Atlantic Ocean.

He was trying to do what no one had ever done—fly alone without stopping from New York to Paris.

Charles Lindbergh had been just a child learning how to walk when the Wright brothers made their first flight. Airplanes had improved so much since then that they had even been used during a world war to drop bombs. But they were nothing like the speedy, sure machines of today, and there weren't very many of them,

either. People in Lindbergh's time stopped and looked up when they heard a plane in the sky.

In 1919 a wealthy New York businessman offered $25,000 to the first person to fly nonstop between New York and Paris. Years passed and the prize remained unclaimed. Lindy meant to win it.

He saved his money to buy a plane, *The Spirit of St. Louis,* and he broke a speed record by flying it from one end of America to the other. When he got to New York he filled the fuel tanks to the top, looked at the weather reports, and stuffed some sandwiches into his jacket pockets. Then he took off for Paris!

The news of Lindy's goal was broadcast over the radio, and people the world over began listening with fear in their hearts to hear where he was. In 1927 an airplane had just one engine, and if that failed, the plane

168

would crash. There were few instruments to help the pilot. The single-engine plane did not have the power to fly high enough to get above dangerous storms.

And Lindbergh ran straight into a storm—a bad one—that night over the ocean. But he was able to go around it. Yet now he was off his course. That meant he had used more gas than he planned. Would his fuel hold out over this almost endless ocean, or would the motor cough and his plane plunge into the water below?

He tried to get back on course, but as the hours passed, Lindy began to wonder more and more if he wasn't far from where he should be. He had taken no radio to help him because he thought it made the plane too heavy. He had absolutely no help from anyone, up there alone in the sky.

Then suddenly he saw something down below in the water! What was it? A fishing boat! He must be close to land—but where? An hour later he knew—Ireland. He was back on course!

Now his biggest problem was one that had been growing with each passing hour—falling asleep! He had been flying for more than thirty hours without sleep—and he had not taken a bite to eat because he was afraid it would make him drowsy.

He fought with every ounce of will that he had, and he succeeded. As he neared his goal, the excitement of triumph helped to keep him awake.

Now reports started rushing to a breathless world. He had been over Ireland; he was now over England; he would soon be over northern France.

And then Lindy landed in Paris!

The world went wild. Lindy was everyone's hero. Almost overnight, they were all singing a song called "Lucky Lindy."

But people didn't admire Lindbergh because he had been lucky. They really loved him because he had made his own "luck." Through bravery and brains, Lindy had proved that—even with luck—the most amazing of machines still needed the brains and bravery of one man to guide it.

F.D.R. and the New Deal

In the summer of 1921, a man was swimming when suddenly he felt very sick. His legs were so heavy that he could hardly get out of the water. He was carried to bed, and a doctor came at once. The doctor examined the man and told him that he would never swim again; he would never even walk again. Franklin D. Roosevelt had *infantile paralysis*, the crippling disease called "polio." Luckily though, F.D.R. was no quitter.

Roosevelt was a popular man in politics, and people were sure that having to spend his life in a wheelchair

171

would end his political career. Franklin Roosevelt was determined not to let a sickness put an end to his active life. Eleven years later he ran for president of the United States, making speeches on crutches and from his wheelchair. And he won!

Franklin Roosevelt could not have chosen a harder time to lead the United States. Because in 1932 America itself was terribly crippled—by poverty. Millions of people were hungry, without jobs, and even homeless. This period of time, now known as the Great Depression, was

the lowest, or "depressed," level of the business cycle, the opposite of good times.

All over America, businesses had to stop making as many products as before. Workers lost their jobs and had far less money to spend. Banks began to close. Then, smaller businesses such as grocery stores and clothing stores began to close because no one could buy the goods. People could not even afford to buy food so farmers had no choice but to leave their farms.

It seemed that the whole free system of American life and business was breaking down. People were hungry, scared, and had nothing to do. There was even talk of revolution. Some people felt that the unfree Russian way would be better. Just as it is today in Soviet Russia, the government tells the people how to live and what to do.

Luckily, most Americans did not want to lose their freedom. But, still something had to be done. As soon as he took office, Roosevelt started a program called the "New Deal." His program called for new laws and new ways to get the factories, banks, and businesses open again. He wanted to get the people in the cities and on the farms back to work. Many people did not like Roosevelt's "New Deal" because it gave so much power to the government. But, it did work to overcome the hard times in America.

So, F.D.R., a man who could not even walk, was able to change the course of American history and get the United States back on its feet again.

The Story of Pearl Harbor

AMERICAN SAILORS WERE RESTING in their barracks on a warm island in the midst of the Pacific Ocean. It was early on a Sunday morning in December of 1941.

The date was December 7th, and the place was Pearl Harbor, Hawaii, an important United States naval base in the Pacific Ocean.

Suddenly the sound of planes was heard!

The bright early morning sun was almost blotted out as swarms of Japanese aircraft darkened the sky. Bombs began dropping by the hundreds.

174

A large group of torpedo planes swooped down once, and then again, and then a third time—and finally one more time! Dozens of dive-bombers flew in wave after wave of destruction—eight waves in all. The attack was so sudden and destruction so swift and heavy that few American planes were able to get into the air to fight back.

Before it was all over, eighty-six American ships had been sunk or made useless, and thousands of men killed and wounded. The United States was now in the Second World War.

How had this war come about?

A man named Adolf Hitler and his Nazi party had taken control of Germany. Thousands of people had been put in prison, and the Nazis had built up a gigantic army. The Germans were better than any other people, Hitler shouted. They must rule the whole world!

Hitler's ally Mussolini, ruler of Italy, had made war on a weak country in Africa, Ethiopia. In the continent of Asia, Japan, another ally of Germany, was attacking China.

In 1939 Germany invaded Poland, and in 1940 the Nazis defeated France. In 1941 Germany invaded Russia. England was being bombed almost daily by Nazi bombers.

America sent tons of supplies to England and other countries fighting the Nazis. The German armies failed to defeat Russia. Germany pleaded with Japan to attack Russia, but the Japanese had other plans. They wanted to expand their own empire in the Pacific first. They decided to begin by attacking American military bases in the Pacific.

The result was that America declared war on Japan and on her allies, Germany and Italy.

To many Americans, it seemed like only yesterday when they had marched off to "make the world safe for democracy" in World War One. Now as they, or their sons, went off again, it was with a grim sadness. Because of Pearl Harbor, every American knew that there would be long years ahead and many lives lost before the world would really be safe for anything.

War Ends—the United Nations Begins

In September of 1945, Japanese leader Mamoru Shigemitsu and American General Douglas MacArthur met face to face on the battleship *U.S.S. Missouri* in Tokyo Bay. Before them lay a set of important documents, one bound in gold, the other bound in black. These papers told the terms of the Japanese surrender. And, when these papers were signed, the most terrible war in history was formally over.

World War Two had affected nearly every country in the world. After Pearl Harbor, the Japanese took over island after island in the Pacific Ocean.

Meanwhile, Hitler and his Axis allies had become stronger and stronger. They had invaded and destroyed many of the countries of Europe, and even the huge country of Russia. As a result, American and Allied troops were fighting all over Europe, the Pacific, Russia, and North Africa.

But, in June of 1944, the American and Allied forces invaded Europe, and slowly but surely won back all the countries Germany had conquered. After six years of terrible fighting, Germany surrendered on May 7, 1945.

Then America devoted itself to defeating Japan. But, because the most destructive weapon in history—the atom bomb—was used, the American victory over Japan did not take very long. On September 2, 1945, the Japanese officials boarded the battleship *Missouri* and surrendered to the United States.

In October of 1945, very soon after World War Two ended, fifty nations joined together to form the United Nations. They had seen millions of people die, great cities destroyed, and economies ruined, all because of war. They wanted peace among all nations, and they wanted to end war forever.

Unfortunately, the United Nations has not kept all people from going to war. It has shortened some wars, and kept other disagreements from becoming destructive battles. People want so much to see an end to war that sometimes they expect the United Nations to do more than it really can.

But, because the UN is more like a peace "club," it has no real power or authority over its members. It can recommend action to a member nation, and also condemn members for doing wrong. But, the members can quit the "club" at any time they wish and then do as they please. But, all United Nations members need the help and friendship of the other nations, so they all try hard to cooperate with each other.

The member countries work together best in programs like UNICEF, to protect the health and welfare of children all over the world. The UN World Health Organization works to eliminate disease and to teach about good health. UNESCO works for world cooperation in science and education, and another organization works for better methods of growing food.

Of course, the countries of the UN are all different in their beliefs. These differences will always cause problems. But, the UN is a place to talk things over. That is why the United Nations offers every country in the world a hope for peace.

Leaders of a New Lifestyle

At the end of World War Two, a famous American general, Dwight D. "Ike" Eisenhower, told a friend that there was nothing he wanted more than to retire from active military service. He was almost 55 years old, and head of the entire U.S. Army.

But, it would be almost 20 years before General "Ike" could retire. He had become so popular with the American people that he was elected to the U.S. presidency by a landslide vote in 1952.

Dwight Eisenhower became president at a very exciting time in America. Things were changing in many ways. Factories and businesses were producing goods as never before. That meant that plenty of jobs were available, so people were able to buy more.

More and more families were able to buy automobiles. Housing areas, called "suburbs," grew up around large cities. Families had more money and more free time.

It was during the 1950's that "push button" appliances became widely available to American families. Television, which had been only an experiment before World War Two, was now a common item in most American homes. With the turn of a dial, a family could bring the world right into its living room.

Even though technology and good times were making life easier for Americans, there were still problems for President Eisenhower and the United States.

One of these problems was what is still known as "The Cold War." This is not an actual "fighting" war, but more of a "war of ideas" between the Communist-controlled countries and the Democratic, or free, nations of the world.

Led by Russia on the Communist side, and by the United States on the Democratic side, these countries greatly distrust each other. This makes it very hard for them to settle their differences.

The Cold War has flared into a real battle several times. The Korean War, which ended in a truce while Eisenhower was president, was one of these flare-ups. There have been others over the years.

Poverty and racial discrimination became problems to be solved in the years after World War Two. In 1954, the U.S. Supreme Court ruled that separate, or segregated,

schools for black and white students were illegal. There was such a fierce argument over this that Eisenhower had to send Federal Troops to go with black students to school in Little Rock, Arkansas in 1957.

Black leaders such as Martin Luther King, Jr. began the idea of "civil rights demonstrations." This form of peaceful protest was meant to bring the cause to public attention. Public protests by many groups were to become a typical news item in the coming years.

The 1960's began with the election of a dynamic, young president, John F. Kennedy. His term of office was cut short when he was assassinated in November of 1963. But, he did much toward solving racial discrimination in America, and in showing the United States strong in its stand against Communism in the Cold War.

One of Kennedy's most famous statements was "Ask not what your country can do for you, ask what you can do for your country." All Americans should ask themselves this question and also be willing to take action.

Kennedy was president during another proud moment of American history. On May 5, 1961, Astronaut Alan B. Shepard made a successful 15-minute space flight—to become America's first man in space. Then, on February 20, 1962, John H. Glenn, Jr. orbited the Earth three times.

America had entered the Space Age, and the world would never be the same again.

A Man on the Moon!

The idea of man walking on the moon once seemed impossible. Then, Astronaut Neil A. Armstrong spoke the words "That's one small step for man, one giant leap for mankind."

It was July 20, 1969 and Armstrong's voice was coming from the moon. He had just stepped from the spaceship *Eagle*. America had become the first country to put a man on the surface of the moon.

Armstrong was soon joined by Astronaut Edwin E. Aldrin, Jr. Together, they spent nearly 2 hours and 15 minutes collecting moon rocks, setting up scientific experiments, and taking photographs.

To make this Apollo 11 Lunar Landing even more exciting, it was televised to a breathless world here on Earth. People watched their TV sets in wonder as the two astronauts bounded around on the moon, enjoying the low gravity that made them almost weightless.

To mark this momentous event, the astronauts left behind a plaque that said "Here Men from the Planet Earth First Set Foot upon the Moon, July 1969, A.D. We Came in Peace for All Mankind." It had been 65 years since the Wright brothers had made their 12-minute flight. But now, man had walked on the moon!

Since this Apollo 11 mission, America has launched five more missions to the moon, and 12 astronauts have walked, worked, and even driven a vehicle on the moon. Once, astronauts even hit a golf ball just to see how far it would go!

The Space Shuttle is the newest manned space mission. Past orbiters could only be used one time. Now, scientists have designed an orbiter that can be used over and over again. The first Space Shuttle is named *Columbia*. It is launched like a rocket, but lands back on Earth like an airplane. So, it can return to Earth to pick up new men and supplies, and then be relaunched into space.

Women are another new feature in the space program. In 1983 Dr. Sally Ride became the first American woman to go into space.

So much waits in the future for America's space program! Astronauts have already lived for many weeks on a space station, *Skylab I*, just to see how weightless space living affects people. Similar space stations, or even the moon itself, may soon become sites for permanent space bases. There, people will conduct tests and experiments, and look through telescopes for a clear view of the universe. These space stations may even become "filling stations" for rockets headed deep into outer space.

America has also sent many spacecraft without astronauts to Mars, Venus, Jupiter, Mercury, and even Saturn to study and photograph their surfaces. Scientists and astronauts know the things that we have learned about our solar system so far are like one small step. They are excited about the future because they know that Armstrong's "giant leap for mankind" was only the first of many to come.

America Today and Tomorrow

On July 4, 1976, America had a big birthday party and every American was invited. There were patriotic parades, colorful fireworks displays, red-white-and blue birthday cakes, and people in Colonial costumes.

It was the 200th Birthday of the Declaration of Independence—the Bicentennial—and people everywhere were celebrating.

To commemorate the signing of the Declaration of Independence, President Gerald Ford rang the Liberty Bell at 2:00 P.M. on July 4, 1976. Americans were happy and thankful to celebrate their freedom.

The Bicentennial Celebration came when Americans seemed to need it the most. The previous years had been very troublesome times.

During the 1960's, American minorities began an energetic and determined demand for equal rights under the law. The Black Americans, Mexican-Americans, American Indians, and other minority groups staged peaceful sit-ins and protests. The age of demands for equality had begun.

But, change came too slowly for some. Riots and other acts of violence broke out in many cities. Protestors, as well as those against the cause of the demonstrators, became violent and destructive. But, the protestors soon realized they were really searching for a new sense of pride in themselves. So, everyone began working together for equality by electing officials in favor of their causes.

The assassinations of Martin Luther King, Jr., a great civil rights leader, and presidential candidate Robert F. Kennedy shocked our country in 1968. We had not yet recovered from President John F. Kennedy's assassination in 1963. These fine men were sincere in their devotion to the welfare of all—equal justice under the law.

188

Over in Southeast Asia, the struggle against Communism was becoming very hard. America became involved in the Vietnam War almost against its will. Many Americans fought and died there because they loved their country and wanted to do what they felt was best for the most people.

Many others protested against this war, making this period in our history even more troubled. In 1973, an agreement was made for a cease-fire and the removal of U.S. troops from South Vietnam.

Honesty is always the best policy. Even the men who run our government make bad mistakes and then they must pay for them. This happened during the Watergate scandal in 1974.

In working to re-elect Richard Nixon as president in 1972, some of the top White House aides approved an illegal break-in of the Democratic National Headquarters in the Watergate Hotel in Washington, D.C. When the break-in burglars were arrested, the aides tried to cover-up their part in the burglary.

Several of these men went to jail for their illegal action. President Nixon resigned his office. In 1973, Vice President Spiro Agnew had also resigned because of illegal income tax practices.

Gerald R. Ford was approved by the Senate as Nixon's Vice President when Agnew resigned. He then became President when Nixon resigned, and chose Nelson Rockefeller as his Vice President.

It was the first time that the U.S. President and Vice President had both been appointed to office instead of being elected by the people. This worried Americans because it had never happened before. But, because our system of government is strong and fair, people found that there was no cause to worry.

In the Bicentennial year of 1976, the American people elected James E. Carter, Jr. of Georgia as their new president. He was a former officer in the U.S. Navy. President Carter served but one term, losing in 1980 to Ronald W. Reagan.

Our history since the founding of our nation has not always been peaceful. Yet the United States, since its beginning, has led the world in the struggle for peace, liberty, and progress for people everywhere. No country can be more proud of its heritage or its accomplishments.

Today and in the future, Americans can stay confident and hopeful in their dedication to the beliefs of their founding fathers.